The Freedom of Forgiveness

THE FREEDOM OF FORGIVENESS

by

DAVID AUGSBURGER

MOODY PRESS

CHICAGO

© 1970, 1988 by
THE MOODY BIBLE INSTITUTE
OF CHICAGO

Original title: *Seventy Times Seven*

Scripture quotations, unless noted otherwise, are from J. B. Phillips's *The New Testament in Modern English* and are used by permission of the Macmillan Company, New York City.

The use of selected references from various versions of the Bible in this publication does not necessarily imply publisher endorsement of the versions in their entirety.

Library of Congress Cataloging in Publication Data

Augsburger, David W.
    Freedom of forgiveness.

    1. Forgiveness—Religious aspects—Christianity.
I. Title.
BV4647.F55A94   1988   234'.5   88-5292
ISBN 0-8024-2884-3

7 9 10 8

Printed in the United States of America

To
The unforgettable few
Who, like their Father,
 Forgive
  And forgive
  And forgive
  And forgive
 Forgetfully
 Freely
At outrageous cost

CONTENTS

PREFACE TO REVISED EDITION

Forgiveness must be one of the deepest human hungers.

Why else would this little book go on passing from hand to hand, being given and received as a gift or used in study groups, year after year?

Eighteen years and more than a half million copies since it was first written, the word about the freedom that forgiveness offers is still useful—and still needed.

At the encouragement of readers, counselors, and pastors who have used it to support reconciliation, we have given it a second life. The book has been rewritten, strengthened, illustrated with further stories from life, and sharpened in its focus on what true forgiveness is about—the regaining of a sister or brother. In Jesus' words, that is the goal of faithful forgiving—not the personal release of private reformation but the interpersonal transformation of relationships.

Forgiveness is something we discover, more than something we do; it is something we gratefully receive, more than something we faithfully give. Perhaps in reading these words on forgiving, you will find the hope of forgiveness becoming more clear, the grace of forgiveness more real, and the experience of forgiveness more precious.

Preface to First Edition

Forgiveness is costly.

Outrageously costly. *Seventy Times Seven* explores a few of the four hundred eighty-nine varieties of hurt where healing can only come from complete forgiveness. The forgiveness that frees both forgiver and forgiven.

Major portions of the material in these chapters appeared first as radio messages on the "Mennonite Hour" broadcast. Wherever possible, quotations have been credited, but many conscious and unconscious references to the writing of others are beyond identification.

My personal gratitude is given to James G. T. Fairfield, editor of *Alive* magazine (published by Mennonite Broadcasts) for his editorial and critical assistance.

And thanks to God for the many people who have shown me in life how to gladly pay the cost of forgiving.

1

I CAN NEVER FORGIVE

"This is it. I'm calling it quits with her! I've had it!"

Having said it aloud to the barren desert, the man —lean, with that stringiness of muscle and etching of face that tell of hard work and time's abrasion—stood up from his rocky seat and began picking his way down the butte to the ranch.

A whole night—a whole decade—of wrestling with frustration, of grappling with anger, lay behind him. Now he would wash his hands of his wife in the quietest way he could.

It had all begun so differently. The tenderness of courtship, those first exploratory expressions of love, the excitement when little Stan was born, then the next two children. The ranch was building itself into security, friendships were knit into a community fabric of acceptance. Their shared faith and life in God was underneath it all.

Then—the first night when she wouldn't talk. So unlike her! How strange the silence was. The children chatted gaily. She wore her favorite smile. But something gray—something glasslike—had risen between them. Something impenetrable, some distance that could never be crossed, though it left him tired from trying.

And her quietness stretched across the months until it seemed, every time he would come into the house from the desert where he ranged the cattle, that their lives were even more deserted, broken only by the prickly irritations of daily friction.

It became too much for them both, so they turned for help. First to their minister, but nothing could break the shell of silence. Then to their doctor, but nothing seemed clear to him; so to a psychiatrist. Nothing opened communication.

Years passed, years in which the silent coexistence slowly embittered their oldest son, driving him away to a job in the East. The scars began to appear in the other children. He spent all the time he could doing things with them—praying, caring, trying to make up for it all.

Then she found a new friend to lean on—a liquid friend. At times, the alcohol made things easier for those few minutes when she passed through the talkative stage and her words would begin a tentative response to the love and acceptance he'd given her through the bitter years.

One night, when she'd had a drop too much, she began to talk. Once started there seemed no stopping. A wistful memory of happiness sparkled through her recollections of those first years together. Then she froze in silence, groping as if against a wall but feeling for some opening, for some crack. He waited, praying. Then, at last, the hidden story surfaced.

There was a man who used to come by the ranch routinely in his work. He'd stop by the house too. For her, it was a friendly break in the lonesome daytime hours with the kids at school. For him, it soon became more. For a while, she laughed off his persuasive advances; but they grew on her, until in a moment of unexpected passion, she yielded herself. Then again, and again. Ten years of festered fear and guilt clouded her face as she told it; then her defiance came back. "But I won't tell you who," she said, "and you can't guess. It's the last person you'd ever suspect."

"Who was it?" he demanded, feeling hatred begin to churn coldly in his viscera. For ten years he had accepted it all; but now, knowing that his worst fears were true, that a betrayal had taken place, he could not stop the spread of anger through him. It took control, and day after day he pressured and prodded, until one night she told him. His best friend.

He sat there stunned, in disbelief. His best friend? The man he'd trusted most? The man who had everything he'd wished for their life? Something soured and died within him. His blood turned bitter.

Oooh, but I'm going to get him, he said to himself, again and again. *I'll burn him in front of his wife. She's a proud one. She'll make it miserable for him. I'll rub him in the dirt until he can't even look up to face a worm.*

All that night he had wandered bitter-blind over the brushy hills and buttes. Now hot with rage, now chilled with hate. Morning found him frozen with revenge. And it was Sunday.

"Why I went to church that morning I'll never know," he told me later. "Something in me I could not hear must have been crying for help. I slipped quietly into the door. And there he stood. His hand out, the same old smile saying his saccharine hello.

"My hand felt frozen to my pocket; I could not get it out. I struggled for what must have been only a fragment of a second but to me it was eternity.

" 'I'll never forgive that man,' I'd vowed again and again through the long bitter night. 'He'll pay for every painful moment I've suffered through ten miserable years.'

"But now, all the hatred my heart held fought with the truth that broke over me as I faced my friend—my enemy.

"The truth I'd prayed automatically a thousand times. 'Forgive me my debts just as I forgive my debtors.' And adding salt were Christ's further words, 'If you will not forgive other people, neither will your heavenly Father forgive you your failures.'

"Then, with a sob in my soul, my hand came out and gripped his. I took the hand of the man who'd betrayed everything I loved. The man who'd stolen our happiness for a few moments' passion. And for the first time I began to understand what it was to forgive. I felt a sense of freedom as the unbearable weight of bitterness began to wash out of me. And I was free. Free to forgive.

"And that new freedom not only gave me the strength to go on; it gave us the resources to find our way through the barrier separating my wife and me. When we could say to each other, 'I accept you just as I did that day we pledged to love and cherish until death,' then healing began its slow change."

"I can never forgive," he had once said. But he discovered a deeper truth about life. That no matter what has been done against you, no matter what hurt has been inflicted, forgiveness is possible.

WHY SHOULD I FORGIVE?

Most of us stall at that point, asking, "Why? Why should I forgive?"

Why shouldn't the person who has wronged me be made to "make things right"—to pay for his sins?

Why shouldn't he be punished? Why shouldn't she suffer?

If any conviction about such things comes naturally, it's the deep-seated belief that "somebody's got to pay."

Forgiveness seems too easy. There should be blood for blood. Eye for eye.

Yes, you can require tooth for tooth in retaliation, but what repayment can you demand from the man who has broken your home or betrayed your daughter? What can you ask from the woman who has ruined your reputation? So few sins can be paid for, and so seldom does the victim possess the power or the advantage to demand payment. In most cases, "making things right" is beyond possibility.

Repayment is impossible!

What of revenge? If you cannot get equal payment or restitution from the offender, at least you can get vengeance. Pay back in kind, tit for tat. Serve the same sauce.

To get even you make yourself even with your enemy. You bring yourself to the same level, and below. There is a saying that goes, "Doing an injury puts you below your enemy; revenging an injury makes you but even; forgiving it sets you above."

Revenge not only lowers you to your enemy's lowest level; what's worse, it boomerangs. One who seeks revenge is like a fool who shoots himself in order to hit his enemy with the kick of the gun's recoil.

Revenge is the most worthless weapon in the world. It ruins the avenger while confirming the enemy in the wrongdoing. It initiates an endless flight down the bot-

tomless stairway of rancor, reprisals, and ruthless retaliation.

Just as repayment is impossible, revenge is impotent!

"What? No repayment? No revenge? But I can
have the soul-satisfaction of hating the wretch!"

Well, yes. You can hate him. You can nurse a grudge
until it grows into a full-blown hate—hoofs, horns, tail,
and all. But hatred harbored grows, spreads, and con-
taminates all other emotions.

Hidden hatred turns trust into suspicion, compassion into caustic criticism, and faith in others into cold
cynicism.

In addition to corroding a disposition, incubated
hatred can elevate blood pressure, ulcerate a stomach,
accelerate stress, or invite a coronary.

Hatred, the wish for another's destruction, is self-
destructive. It is cheaper to pardon than to resent. The
high cost of anger, the extravagant expense of hatred,
and the unreasonable interest on grudges make resentment out of the question!

It is wiser to begin working toward forgiveness before the sting has begun to swell. Before the molehill
mushrooms into a mountain. Before bitterness like an
infection—or rigor mortis—sets in.

What a strange thing bitterness is! It breaks on us
when we need it least, when we're down and in desperate need of all our freedom, ability, and energy to get
back up.

And what strange things bitterness can do to us. It
slowly sets, like a permanent plaster cast, perhaps pro-
tecting the wearer from further pain but ultimately
holding the sufferer rigid in frozen animation. Feelings
and responses have turned to concrete. Bitterness is
paralysis.

A young man, falsely accused, condemned, and penalized by his high school principal, turns sullen, angry, and bitter. His faith in justice and authority dies. He will not forgive.

A girl, betrayed by a fellow she trusted, is forced, becomes pregnant, then turns bitter and withdrawn. Her faith in humanity ends. She cannot forgive.

A woman, deserted by her husband, left to be both mother and father to their two sons, turns angry at life—at the whole universe. Her faith in God and everything good has ended. She did not forgive.

Bitterness is such a potent paralysis of mind, soul, and spirit that it can freeze reason and emotion. Our attitudes turn cynical, uncaring, critical, and caustic. Where we once ventured to place faith in others, now we trust no one. Optimism darkens to pessimism. Faith grays into doubt.

We withdraw, turtlelike, into our protective shells of bitter distrust. We've been burned once, and, once burned, we become twice shy.

Letting bitterness seal us in can be a useful excuse for acting irresponsibly. Being responsible in any painful situation usually calls for us to accept our part of the blame for the way things are. But being bitter about it can save all that. We can scapegoat others. We may even feel justified in blaming God for our troubles and difficulties. (Remember man's first impulse when in trouble. Blame God. Adam blamed the woman first —and then the Creator.)

Bitterness is a cyclical, repetitive, tightly closed circle of self-centered pain. It carries us around and around the same senseless arc, around and around ourselves. Like a child learning to ride a bicycle, knowing how to ride but not how to stop, we pedal on and on, afraid to quit, yet wishing desperately for someone to come and take the bars, break our circling, and let us off. Bitterness is useless. Repayment is impossible. Revenge is impotent. Resentment is impractical.

Only forgiveness can reconcile the differences and restore healing to a relationship. Rejecting all relationships that have failed us is the most common "solution" in our contemporary Western culture, among Christians and non-Christians alike. Cut off the old connections, withdraw from all interactions, live at a distance, avoid intimacy or involvement. Above all, do not risk working at forgiveness.

As common as this option is, it is destructive of human relationships, it fragments personality, it is inconsistent with the basic values of any faith commitment.

Only if you have no need for forgiveness yourself do you dare consider hesitating to forgive another. The two go hand in hand.

"If you forgive other people their failures, your Heavenly Father will also forgive you. But if you will not forgive . . . neither will your Heavenly Father forgive you your failures" (Matthew 6:14-15).

"I'll never forgive," General James Oglethorpe said to John Wesley.

"Then I hope, sir," replied Wesley, "you never sin!"

George Herbert once wrote, "One that cannot forgive others breaks the bridge over which all must pass if they would ever reach heaven; for everyone has need to be forgiven." Forgiving and being forgiven are all of one piece. They cannot be separated. In giving we receive. In accepting those who have injured us we open ourselves to God's acceptance.

It is not a matter of which comes first. There is no sequence of time or priority. The two are one. Anyone who loves God must also love his neighbor. Anyone who hates another does not and cannot love God. Love of God and our neighbor are interlocking and indivisible. We only learn to love as we learn to know God. And we truly learn to know God as we learn to love our brother and sister. It's all of a piece. The life that is open to the love of God is loving to others. The person who truly receives the forgiveness of God is truly forgiving of others.

To be forgiven of God for our daily trespasses (and how desperately each of us needs His forgiveness), we must forgive, accept, and love.

God's forgiveness gives us the freedom to love and live creatively. The rush of God's strength, which brings forgiveness, gives in turn the ability to forgive, and forgive, and forgive, not just seven times, as the apostle Peter once volunteered, but seventy times seven, as Christ taught in an unforgettable story (Matthew 18:21-35).

A certain poor man owed his king more than two million dollars. He couldn't pay, so the king ordered the man, his wife, children, and property sold to pay the debt.

The man, face in the dust, pleaded with the king, "Oh, sir, be patient! I'll pay it all."

"Two million dollars?" asked the king. But then, in pity, he forgave him all his debt.

The man, overjoyed, left the king. Outside he met a neighbor who owed him twenty dollars.

"Pay up," he demanded.

"Just be patient, and I'll have it for you next week."

"Nothing doing," says the man and has him thrown in debtors' prison.

The king gets wind of it all and summons the man to him again. "You evil wretch," he says, "here I canceled that tremendous debt for you, and you have the gall to be unforgiving over a few dollars. You have sentenced yourself! To jail!"

Then said Jesus to His listeners, "That's how My heavenly Father will treat you, unless each of you forgives your brother from your heart."

The contrast between our debt to God and the debts others may owe us is immeasurable.

And when God has forgiven us the debt we owe Him, how can we be unforgiving to others who owe us so little in comparison?

Anything you may need to forgive is only a shadow of the debt you have been forgiven.

Forgive? Till seventy times seven!

2

THEN WHAT IS FORGIVENESS?

"I had a brother once, and I betrayed him."

With these words, African writer Laurens Van der Post begins a profound human drama in his book *The Seed and the Sower* (New York: Morrow, 1963).

Once there were two brothers from a small South African village. The elder brother was tall, handsome, intelligent, an excellent athlete, a good student, and a natural leader. Sent away to a private school, he quickly made a name for himself. As an admired campus leader and outstanding athlete, he was in his final year when his younger brother arrived to begin studies.

The brother was not good-looking or athletic. He was a hunchback. Since his childhood his mother had sewed padded jackets that concealed his spinal deformity. His sensitivity to his short, curved stature had grown through the years. None of the family spoke of it in respect for his shamed feelings. Yet the boy had one great gift. He had a magnificent voice and could sing gloriously, like a nightingale on the veld.

Soon after his arrival at the private school, the students held initiation ceremonials, which consisted of some public humiliation to extract proof of courage. Often one student would be singled out to be especially hounded as a kind of scapegoat. On the eve of the initiation, the student body in a cruel mob action ganged up on the younger brother, carried him off to the water tank, and demanded that he sing. When he sang so frighteningly beautifully in his fear, they became all the more abusive, and tore off his shirt to reveal his never-before-seen hunchback to public ridicule.

The older brother was aware of what was happening; he could have gone out and faced the sadistic mob. A word from him would have put a stop to the whole tragic scene. As a leader, he could have acknowledged the strange boy as his brother, but instead he busied himself in his work in the laboratory while the mob raged outside. He betrayed his brother by refusing to go out to him in love when he was being abused.

The brother survived physically, but his spirit was crushed. He withdrew into himself. He never sang again. At the end of the term he returned to the family farm. Keeping to himself, he lived a lonely, reclusive life.

The older brother rose to successful prominence in the capital, and when World War II came was an officer stationed in Palestine. One night, recovering from an injury, he lay under the stars and in a dream saw himself as Judas in the circle of disciples around the Christ. "I am Judas; I had a brother once, and I betrayed him," he said.

"Go to your brother," Christ replied.

The journey from Palestine was incredibly difficult. He arrived unannounced and found his brother watering plants in the parched garden. It was a time of long drought.

He looked into his brother's dark eyes, still imprisoned in the painful past. The moment of time arrested was visible in his face as well as in his twisted form.

"I've come all this distance to spend a few hours with you," he said, then went straight to the heart of the matter of his great wrong. When he had finished, both were in tears. The first rainstorm of the year was breaking as the older brother walked back to the house and the younger turned off the irrigation water.

Then in the distance he heard the song of his brother in the garden, as he had not heard him sing since childhood. A song of his own writing in boyhood, but now with a new verse.

> I rode all through the night
> to the fire in the distance burning
> And beside the fire found
> He who had waited for so long.

"Go to your brother," said Jesus, "and if he will hear you, you have regained your brother." For Jesus, this is the goal—the central focus, the true meaning of forgiveness. The primary issue is not inner peace for oneself, not moral rightness with one's own conscience, not assurance of one's own salvation. These are self-centered, narcissistic goals that are only further evidence of the fact that one is still taking care of predominately one's own needs, not caring for the relationship or for the pain in the other.

In modern Western thought, writing on forgiveness is almost exclusively focused on the process within, the virtues of the freedom found by the forgiver. It is common for teaching on forgiveness to never get to what Jesus spoke of and to deal only with the prerequisite steps of seeing the other person as having worth again and restoring perceptions of love. Unfortunately most writing on forgiveness in Western Christianity could omit the word and speak only of love, since, in New Testament terms, that is all that is addressed. If being able to love the offender or the offended once more were all that is needed, then both could take the step of attitudinal change in the privacy of their closet or heart and go on without deeper conversation about repentance and change in reconstructing the relationship.

But that is not what Jesus intended. "If your brother has a grievance against you, go to him" (Matthew 5:23, paraphrase). "If you have something against your brother, go to him" (Matthew 18:15, paraphrase). "If your brother sins, confront him" (Luke 17:3, paraphrase).

These are Jesus' central words on working through injury and working out forgiveness. They do not describe desirable consequences of forgiveness as we commonly hear taught, but the central and unavoidable process. We are not even beginning the process of forgiving and being forgiven until we take the first steps in attempting to restore, reconstruct, and rediscover a relationship.

"Forgiveness" in the New Testament context is more synonymous with our usage of "reconciliation" than with "love." The two Greek words for forgiveness are translated most clearly as "to release or set free" and "to offer a gift of grace." Word studies done on these words apart from context, usage, story, and setting allow Western individualists to define forgiveness as a private releasing of another, a personal gift of grace within the believer's heart. But in the context, the meaning is always relational; it is addressing the actual interactions between offended people. We are called to "forgive as God in Christ has forgiven" (Colossians 3:13, paraphrase; cf. Ephesians 4:32)—and that is not a detached private pardon or release. God's forgiveness in Jesus was utterly, totally invested in incarnate involvement, crucified self-commitment, life-blood contact with us humans. There is no cheap forgiveness in Christ who is our example, model, and empowerment.

THE CHRIST OF THE CROSS

The cross shows how difficult it was for God to forgive, how far God was willing to go to forgive, and how costly it is to forgive.

Dorothy Sayers describes it:

> Hard it is, very hard,
> To travel up the slow and stony road
> To Calvary, to redeem mankind; far better
> To make but one resplendent miracle,
> Lean through the cloud, lift the right hand of
>   power
> And with a sudden lightning smite the world
>   perfect.
> Yet this was not God's way, Who had the power,
> But set it by, choosing the cross, the thorn,
> The sorrowful wounds. Something there is,
>   perhaps,
> That power destroys in passing, something
>   supreme,
> To whose great value in the eyes of God
> That cross, that thorn, and those five wounds
>   bear witness.[1]

Why this talk about God on a cross? Because God accepted the cross to both make forgiveness possible and to model forgiving to an unforgiving world.

The Christ of the cross is our great example. Christ suffered for you, leaving you an example, that you should follow His steps, wrote the apostle Peter (1 Peter 2:21).

1. Dorothy Sayers, "The Devil to Pay," in *Masterpieces of Religious Verse* (New York: Harper, 1948), p. 189.

In Jesus we see compassion modeled. We see love embodied. We see faithfulness to truth carried to its authentic conclusion. We see human possibilities beyond our own experience. We see the face of God, and it is a face of forgiving love.

Of course we need more than an example to live by, we need the power to live in new ways. Just admiring beauty will not make us beautiful; just respecting an example of goodness will not improve our character. We need help that can set us free to be like Him. We need the transforming relationship that is at the heart of forgiveness.

The Christ of the cross is the greatest moral influence. Jesus said, "I, if I be lifted up . . . , will draw all men unto me" (John 12:32, KJV*). Christ's self-sacrifice was not "just a great example." It is the kind of scalding humility that makes us thoroughly ashamed of ourselves and our self-centered living. It is a display of such unlimited love that makes us sick of our unloving inhumanity to one another. It is the kind of compassion that really shows us up as the sinners we all are and breaks up our rebellious spirit. The moral influence of His act changes our attitude toward God. In gratitude we live for Him. His virtuous life and action was lived in relationships with others that modeled deep reconciliation and forgiveness.

Yet there is much more. Jesus was not just a fantastically good and righteous folk hero who died nobly, unjustly, and tragically to show us the highest good. His death had a greater, more personal effect on our lives. It is relationally connected to our inner ledgers of guilt, shame, and anxiety before God and others.

The Christ of the cross is our great Substitute. If there is any justice in this universe, if God is a God of

*King James Version.

justice who loves what's right and fair, then God cannot overlook human inhumanity, murder, rebellion, selfishness, and all the rest of the evil that we do and are.

Who of us could ever live well enough to merely
even up his own score? No, the debt we owe God for
our insulting refusal to live right and for our rebellion
against love is beyond us all. Such an infinitely vast
debt only God could pay. But God doesn't owe it. We
owe the debt we cannot pay.

God paid the debt He did not owe.

God became human—a divine Human—in Jesus
Christ to stand with us in our evil. To pay the immeasurable price. To pay for what you and I have done in
choosing to be what we all are—sinners! "At just the
right time, when we were still powerless, Christ died
for the ungodly" (Romans 5:6, NIV*). "He himself
bore our sins in his body on the tree" (1 Peter 2:24,
NIV).

*The Christ of the cross is our Forgiver and our for-
giveness.* Jesus Christ became our reconciliation. He re-
connects us to God.

When God forgave us, God did not wink at our sin
and overlook it. God took our lostness in sin so serious-
ly that He went all the way to Calvary to substitute
Himself for us, to die in our place, to pay the price of
forgiving such a vast debt.

The cross shows how difficult it was for God to forgive.

"God was in Christ personally reconciling the
world to himself" (2 Corinthians 5:19).

This was no scapegoating! This isn't an ugly story
of God's punishing Jesus for our sins. Morally and justly the guilt of one's sins cannot be transferred to a third
party. It must be settled between the two involved.

*New International Version.

Either the sinner bears his own guilt (that's cold justice); the one sinned against, the first party, may absorb what the second party did (that's sacrifice); or the two may meet in transforming repentance and redemption. That's forgiveness.

And that's what God did in Christ at Calvary. He tasted death for everyone (Hebrews 2:9) in sacrifice; He identified with us in incarnation, life, ministry, and in His ongoing life in the church. He has fully encountered humankind in forgiving love as well as forgiving integrity. Grace and truth came to us in Jesus Christ (John 1:14). The gracious acceptance blended with truthful confrontation invites healing and growth. Both are essential in working through to true forgiveness.

Authentic forgiveness is the mutual recognition that repentance is genuine and right relationships are achieved. Forgiving requires the grace to accept the other as an equal partner in the search for reconciliation and the genuineness to give repentance or to respond to another's repentance with full trust and respect. Grace and truth, acceptance and confrontation, sacrifice and prophetic rebuke are needed in resolving alienation, injustice, or interpersonal injuries.

In forgiveness we go to the sister; we seek out the brother; we rediscover each other. That is the goal of forgiveness. It was God's way with us, it must be our way with each other. We are to forgive one another as God in Christ has forgiven us.

Forgiveness is not finally complete until the severed friendship is mended. And the new weld of forgiveness should afterward result in a deeper, stronger union than existed before!

The final step in forgiving is to do something to heal the wound until nothing remains but the forgotten scar.

Forgiveness is acceptance with no exception. It accepts not only the hurt you've received, it accepts the one who did the hurting, and it accepts the loss caused by the hurtful actions or words.

Seven times a day. In fact, seventy times seven.

3

How Can I Forgive?

"I'll never forget the look of white anger, shame, and terror that filled Lori's eyes that night," the mother told me.

"When she came through the door, all disheveled and distraught, I knew what had happened—what I had feared for weeks had become an awful reality.

"You see, it all started when Lori, our only child, and—pardon this from a mother—a lovely woman, began dating this fellow. Suddenly, friends who'd never interfered before were stopping by to drop a word of warning. No one gave details, just a lot of vague caution. We tried to dissuade Lori, but our opposition only drove them closer and closer. Then one night their intimacies accelerated, Lori tried to stop it, he grew violent, forced her, dropped her off a block from home, and fled town—leaving her guilt ridden, depressed, violated, and pregnant.

"Finally, through his mother, we discovered that he was with his estranged father in another city. They brought him back. He acted repentant enough and asked to see her alone to talk things out. Instead, he became violent again, this time beating her severely before he was restrained.

"Lori was hospitalized with severe concussion and shock. For days in deep depression, she wanted to die.

"The boy? Two weeks' detention, a few interviews with a doctor, and he was free. Now today I learn that he's got an acquaintance's daughter pregnant, and they're getting married.

"I lie awake at night, burning with anger and bitterness. True, Lori's recovering from it all. The baby's been adopted into a fine home, the social worker says. Lori's going to enter college in another state to get away from it all. But the scars go deep to her soul. The old buoyancy and trust are gone out of her. And when I see it, I feel everything in my own soul turning to hate.

"I can't express the feelings I have toward this—this—*thing* who ruined our lives. Isn't there some way I can heal the hurt of all this?

"Is there no forgiveness for things this big and terrifying? If there is, how, *how* do I begin?"

How do you forgive? Forgive when the cost is staggering, the pain unbearable, and your own anger still swelling?

You need all the strength you can absorb from God in order to love and forgive. You need the potency of prayer, the power of His compassion within you, and cooperation with His healing touch.

The secret is God working within and you working it out in life. He works within you; you work it out in heart and mind.

"Work out the salvation that God has given you with a proper sense of awe and responsibility. For it is God who is at work within you, giving you the will and the power to achieve his purpose" (Philippians 2:12-13).

Where do you begin when it's the most difficult work of all? You begin with understanding.

UNDERSTANDING THE OTHER

Forgiveness begins with a discovery—a discovery of both understanding and of the capacity to be understanding.

Understanding is something we discover. The discovery often begins with seeing that another's behavior has its roots in the person's past, in his inner pain, in the problems of living that have contributed to the injury between you.

There is a reason behind every action. If a man is boorish and rude, it may be that he is still a child, unable to grow up.

If a woman is demanding, possessive, or even exploitative of others, she may be a little lost girl, grasping desperately for affection and acceptance.

"To know all is to forgive all" is an ancient proverb housing a half-truth. Understanding underlies forgiveness. But that's only half the truth.

Because even perfect understanding of any other person might breed contempt, not forgiveness. Any human understanding of another human is tainted with our own evil. None of us is good enough to be entrusted with complete knowledge about another.

But that's impossible to begin with. You can't come to know another person bit by bit and cell by cell.

That's not the purpose of understanding at all. The real purpose is only to help us see the difference between what the person *did* and what the person *is!* Although someone has done wrong, there is more to him than that single misdeed.

Beyond the discovery that we can begin to understand the other person lies a second discovery. Where we cannot understand, it is still possible to be under-standing.

Our best intentioned attempts "to understand" that lead us to try deciphering the other person's for-mula, to attempt unraveling the mysterious tangle of emotions and motivations, can become an exercise in hypocritical superiority. We are tempted to start im-pugning others' motives, prejudging their attitudes and actions, and stereotyping them into some set of cubby-holes that we've constructed—classifying and perma-freezing them into neat categories. Playing God.

In being understanding we accept the complexity of human motivation, the contradictions in persons that are beyond our explanation. We realize that there are ambivalences and inner tensions we will not be able to explain, but we can embrace in the arms of under-standing, complex and terrifying as they often are. This capacity to be understanding of what is beyond under-standing is something we value in others, and it's what others often value in us. Paul wrote that love—being understanding—is greater than great insight. "Even though you understand all mysteries and all knowledge but have not love, you are nothing" (paraphrase; see 1 Corinthians 13).

Any offender, whatever the offense, deserves the gift of understanding. We can go beyond reacting to what others do or how they act and begin responding to what they are, to what they want to be, or what they could become.

Does this mean agreeing with everything they say and do? No, although some who cry for understanding often believe so. Like the young man who voiced this to me as he criticized his dad: "He doesn't understand me, or else he'd see things the same way I do."

True? Not really. It may be that the dad disagrees because he understands all too well. Understanding need not be agreement. Rather than agreeing with, it's seeing with, seeing things from the other's point of view whether you believe it valid or not. It may also be feeling with, responding to the other's emotional reactions whether they seem reasonable to you or not. Understanding is not unconditional acceptance, but it is acceptance in any condition, in any situation.

That is the beginning point for working out forgiveness in life. We must then take the second step of forgiveness.

VALUING OTHERS

Look again at an unforgivable man.

He is a man. The highest unit of value in the universe is a human soul (Mark 8:36-37).

He is a man *for whom Christ died.* No one for whom Christ died can be to me an enemy, an object of hate or scorn. God valued each person more highly than He valued His own life. If I love God, how can I keep from loving my sister or brother (1 John 4:20)?

He is a man for whom Christ died, *meant to be a child of God.* He has the possibility of becoming a saint as well as a demon. He could be right—right with God and man if it were not for the wrong decisions made, the wrong circumstances that supported them, and the wrong actions that followed.

No one (however irresponsible) is too low to be an object of God's love.

No one (however evil) is excluded from the forgiveness of God, except as one excludes himself by unrepentance.

No one can be considered worthless when Christ— God Himself—died for him or her.

No one is unlovable—if God loves her, then God can love her through me!

LOVING OTHERS

The third step toward forgiveness is loving others. Before the real work of forgiveness can begin, understanding and valuing must be expressed in restoring perceptions of love. To love is to see the other as precious regardless of the wrong done or the injury felt.

Ralf Luther writes: "To love one's enemy does not mean to love the mire in which the pearl lies, but to love the pearl that lies in the mire."[1]

By seeing the other with new eyes, by restoring perceptions of worth, by recognizing the other's preciousness in spite of a particular behavior, you can glimpse the pearl glinting through the mire.

I know a woman who discovered this truth the hard way.

Her husband is trapped by chronic alcoholism.

"How can you keep on loving and forgiving?" I once asked her.

"It happened late one night," she said. "He had come home drunk, cursing, and abusive.

"It was when I faced his glassy-eyed stare. He lifted his hand to strike at me, and hatred, anger, and revulsion flared up within me.

"Then I remembered—was it a kind word spoken in our courtship, the tenderness of our wedding vows, his believing prayer when our son was born? I don't know, but right there I knew that the man I used to know and love was the *real* man, not this one before me.

"Now I cannot look at him without seeing the empty, desperate captivity that holds him.

"My forgiveness and love are his only link to God. How could I withhold it?"

1. Ralf Luther, as cited in Helmut Thielicke, *Life Can Begin Again* (Philadelphia: Fortress, 1963), p. 75.

There! See? In the mud of his captivity, she sees the gleam of pearl! When we have learned to look about us with the loving eyes of Christ, no one is unlovable, none beyond compassion.

Forgiveness is both an assertion and an affirmation.

As an assertion, we face the unhealthy, destructive, ill-motivated, unacceptable behavior head on. We do not condone the offense or overlook the wrong done, but we refuse to consider this behavior as a measure of what the person is in his or her deepest self. We assert that this person has worth no matter what choices, actions, or mixed intentions are visible.

We affirm the healthy, the constructive, the right-motivated, the responsible center of the person. We choose to affirm and to believe that this is the real, the possible, the capable, and accountable core of the person. We claim and reclaim the real center no matter what has surfaced in our relationship.

What was done is separated from who has done it. In working through our mutual repentance, mutual change of attitudes, mutual reconstruction of the relationship, this assertion and this affirmation go hand in hand, step by step. We step forward on one assertive foot, gain balance, then place forward the affirmation. Often this happens in small but increasing increments, step by step, until the journey of restoring love, recognizing repentance, reclaiming relationship, and reopening the future has been completed.

Understanding, valuing, loving are all steps toward forgiveness. They are not yet forgiving, but the prerequisite steps toward forgiveness. The real work of forgiving begins when an attitude of love has been restored. Then the negotiations of trust can begin resolving anger, suspicion, and resentment and reopening the future. This is the difficult task that gets bypassed when forgiveness is made cheap, private, and one-way. Real forgiveness is more costly, more demanding, more deep. Real forgiveness comes with the recovery of a relationship, even when the rupture is repeated again and again.

Forgiveness can happen seventy times seven.

4

LEARNING TO FORGIVE

It was in a church in Munich that I saw him—a balding, heavyset man in a gray overcoat, a brown felt hat clutched between his hands. It was 1947 and I had come from Holland to defeated Germany with the message that God forgives.

And that's when I saw him, working his way forward against the others. One moment I saw the overcoat and the brown hat; the next, a blue uniform and a visored cap with its skull and crossbones. It came back with a rush: the huge room with its harsh overhead lights; the pathetic pile of dresses and shoes in the center of the floor; the shame of walking naked past this man. I could see my sister's frail form ahead of me, ribs sharp beneath the parchment skin. *Betsie, how thin you were!*

Betsie and I had been arrested for concealing Jews in our home during the Nazi occupation of Holland; this man had been a guard at Ravensbruck concentration camp.

Now he was in front of me, hand thrust out: "A fine message, Fraulein! How good it is to know that, as you say, all our sins are at the bottom of the sea!"

And I, who had spoken so glibly of forgiveness, fumbled in my pocketbook rather than take that hand. He would not remember me, of course—how could he remember one prisoner among those thousands of women?

But I remembered him and the leather crop swinging from his belt. I was face-to-face with one of my captors and my blood seemed to freeze.

"You mentioned Ravensbruck in your talk," he was saying. "I was a guard in there." No, he did not remember me.

"But since that time," he went on, "I have become a Christian. I know that God has forgiven me for the cruel things I did there, but I would like to hear it from your lips as well. Fraulein"—again the hand came out —"will you forgive me?"

And I stood there—I whose sins had every day to be forgiven—and could not. Betsie had died in that place—could he erase her slow terrible death simply for the asking?

It could not have been many seconds that he stood there, hand held out, but to me it seemed hours as I wrestled with the most difficult thing I had ever had to do.

For I had to do it—I knew that. The message that God forgives has a prior condition: that we forgive those who have injured us. "If you do not forgive men their trespasses," Jesus says, "neither will your Father in heaven forgive your trespasses."

I knew it not only as a commandment of God, but as a daily experience. Since the end of the war I had had a home in Holland for victims of Nazi brutality.

Those who were able to forgive their former enemies were able also to return to the outside world and rebuild their lives, no matter what the physical scars. Those who nursed their bitterness remained invalids. It was as simple and as horrible as that.

And still I stood there with the coldness clutching my heart. But forgiveness is not an emotion—I knew that too. Forgiveness is an act of the will, and the will can function regardless of the temperature of the heart.

Even as the angry, vengeful thoughts boiled through me, I saw the sin of them. Jesus Christ himself had died for this man; was I going to ask for more? *Lord Jesus*, I prayed, *forgive me and help me to forgive him.*

I tried to smile. I struggled to raise my hand. I could not. I felt nothing, not the slightest spark of warmth or charity. And so again I breathed a silent prayer.

Jesus. I cannot forgive him. Give me your forgiveness.

As I took his hand, mechanically, woodenly, a most incredible thing happened. From my shoulder along my arm and through my hand a current seemed to pass from me to him, while into my heart sprang a love for this stranger that almost overwhelmed me.

And so I discovered that it is not on our forgiveness any more than on our goodness that the world's healing hinges, but on His. When He tells us to love our enemies, He gives along with the command, the love itself.[1]

*   *   *

No matter how often we have forgiven or have been forgiven by others, we are all still learning to for-

1. Corrie Ten Boom, *Tramp for the Lord* (Old Tappan, N.J.: Revell, 1974), pp. 53-55.

give. Forgiveness is not a skill that is mastered and becomes second nature. It must be faced each time injury or injustice strikes.

Forgiveness is not a gift one claims, internalizes, and then possesses for life. It must be rediscovered in each situation of pain. We never grow beyond the learning stage, we never go beyond the level of student.

No one is a master here. We are learning to love unconditionally; we are discovering how to work out the conditions of forgiveness.

In Corrie Ten Boom's open confession of anger and love, of resentment and release, the steps of forgiveness are visible in the compressed tension of a surprising confrontation.

Forgiveness is not an act—it is a process. It is not a single transaction—it is a series of steps. Beware of any view of instant, complete, once-for-all forgiveness. Instant solutions tend to be the ways of escape, of avoidance, or of denial, not of forgiveness. Forgiveness takes time—time to be aware of one's feelings, alert to one's pain and anger, open to understand the other's perspective, willing to resolve the pain and reopen the future.

The steps of forgiveness are:

1. *Restoring the attitude of love.* To love another is to see that person as full of worth and precious regardless of any wrongdoing. This is not forgiveness, although most writers and pastors call it such. It is the prerequisite step. Forgiving cannot begin until love has been re-extended to the offender. Love is possible when we see the other's value once more, recognize his preciousness, and choose to be understanding, even of what is beyond being understood.

2. *Releasing the painful past.* To accept another is to meet him or her now, as the person he really is. To hold the past between us as if it can be undone or to demand that what was done must be redone is fantasy not reality. To come to terms with reality is to accept the past as past. Obviously, what has happened has happened, but emotionally it is still taking place. In anger we struggle with the illusion that we can turn time backwards and run it all through again, that we can make the other undo what he or she did. I am not my past; I am a person capable of repenting, changing, and turning away from past patterns of behavior. You are not your past; you are equally free to change if you accept the freedom that is within you. To affirm that freedom is the first step of forgiveness.

3. *Reconstructing the relationship.* This is the real work of forgiveness. To review the pain of offense within each of us and between us is not easy, but it is the way to healing. As we work through our anger and pain in reciprocal trusting and risking, at last we come to recognize the genuineness of each other's intentions. Our repentance needs to be authentic, honest, and as complete as possible at the moment. That is the central work of forgiveness. "If your brother wrongs you, rebuke him; and if he repents, forgive him. Even if he wrongs you seven times in a day and comes back to you seven times saying, 'I am sorry,' you are to forgive him," says Jesus in His most succinct and clear description of essential forgiveness (Luke 17:3-4, NEB*).

4. *Reopening the future.* As we begin to cancel our angry demands on the present in the previous step, we

*New English Bible.

begin to drop our demands on the future. The demand for ironclad guarantees that will fix all future acts permanently and securely and insure our safety from any future pain must be canceled. No one can offer such assurance and go on living as a truly human being. Such promises of perfection are possible only for saints or statues, and neither are desirable in a relationship. In the future we will be spontaneous together. We may fail. We may act hurtfully again.

5. *Reaffirming the relationship.* Reconciliation must end in celebration, or the process has not ended. We must touch each other as deeply as is possible in our release of the pain and celebrate the mutual recognition that right relationship has now been restored or achieved. This bonding of renewed acceptance and mutual affirmation allows us to meet with a new meaning to our relationship. To end a reconciliation negatively —"May God help us that this never happens again"— blocks our growth as persons. It is fascinating that the words of mistrust and suspicion Jacob and Laban set between them—"May the Lord watch between you and me, when we are parted from each other's sight" (Genesis 31:49, NEB)—have been transformed in following generations into a benediction of love and a celebration of relationship.

FORGIVING, FORGETTING, FORGOING

Reflecting on Corrie Ten Boom's marvelous story, we may ask, Did she forgive the prison guard? No. She took all the steps possible at that moment, but she herself describes it as steps one and two. Love was extended, the past was recognized as past. Before real forgiveness could take place, the two would need to remember the pain together, recall the injury together, recognize real repentance together, and agree to forget together.

Theologian Frank Stagg writes insightfully about authentic forgiveness:

> Forgiving and forgetting are related, but forgiving precedes forgetting. To forgive, one must first remember the injury, the impact, the injustice done.
>
> To forget ignores the needs of the offender and injures the offended by driving the sense of being wronged deep into one's own being where resentment does its slow destructive work. Forgetting is negative, passive; forgiving is positive and creative.
>
> Before one can forgive and forget, both offender and offended must remember together, recall the wrongdoing together, finish the feelings together, reconstruct the relationship together and then they may forget together. In the remembering, reconstructing, forgiving and forgetting each regains the other.[2]

To insist that forgetting comes first is to make passing the final exam the entrance requirement for the course! How often have you been told to "forget and forgive" and then kicked yourself because you couldn't? The more you tried to forget, the better your memory!

Just as with insomnia, the more you attempt to stop the mad race of thoughts, the swifter they fly. The person who struggles blindly to forget only sears the thought more deeply into the memory.

Forgetting is the *result* of complete forgiveness; it is never the *means*. It is the final step, not the first.

To say, "I can forgive, but I can't forget," is really saying, "I know how to overlook a wrong but not to forgive it."

2. Frank Stagg, *Polarities of Man's Existence in Biblical Perspective* (Philadelphia: Westminster, 1973), p. 161.

Now, let's be clear—forgetful forgiveness is not a case of holy amnesia that erases the past. Instead, it is the experience of healing that draws the poison from the wound.

You may recall the hurt, but you will not relive it. No constant reviewing, no rehashing of the old hurt, no going back to sit on the old gravestones where past grievances lie buried.

True, the hornet of memory may fly again, but forgiveness has drawn its sting. The curse is gone. The memory is powerless to arouse or anger. It was said of Lincoln, "His heart had no room for the memory of a wrong." Forgetting follows forgiving.

Not that the past is changed as a result.

The past is the past. Nothing can alter the facts. What has happened has happened forever. But the meaning can be changed. That is one part of *forgiveness*.

To "for-give" is, in the English language, an extended, expanded, strengthened form of the verb *to give*. By intensifying the verb we speak of giving at its deepest level, of self-giving, of *giving forth* and *giving up* deeply held parts of the self.

To "for-give" is a process of *giving up*. In forgiving we give up demands for perfect behavior, perfect justice, perfect resolution, perfect retribution. All we can ask is genuine repentance of ourself and of the other. In forgiving we give up the angry picture of the wrongdoer. We put aside the view of the other as an unworthy, unacceptable, unforgivable offender. In forgiving we lay aside the view of ourselves as righteous and the other as totally unrighteous, and we begin to experience the truth that we are both fallible humans in need of being forgiven.

To "for-give" is a process of giving forth. In forgiving we give a new trust to another exemplified by our risking being open, vulnerable, and available again. We allow the future to come meet us without constricting its flow through ironclad guarantees of perfection or fearfully frozen limitations on our spontaneity. In forgiving we give forth a new freedom by believing in the other, by accepting fully the genuine worth and intrinsic value of this person who is as much a child of God as we are.

In giving up, we forgo revenge and forfeit recriminations; we forbid old resentment and forbear strategies of getting satisfaction for the injury. In giving forth we foresee an open future in our relationship; what we cannot foreknow we can still foretell out of our commitment to forgive. In forgiving we forsake old patterns of brooding review and move toward forgetting the pain and remembering the healing. In forgiving and forgetting we forge a new relationship.

By using the series of intensified words that begin with *for*, although there are many more, we are recognizing the depth of effort, feeling, and commitment required in the work of forgiveness.

FORGIVENESS IS RARE, HARD, COSTLY

"Will I forgive you? Why, of course! I've already forgiven you. Forget it, it didn't matter!"

The man had come to me with a serious apology. And what did I say to him? "It didn't bother *me*. I couldn't have cared less about what happened back there."

What did I mean by that? Was I trying to tell him his actions and insults couldn't hurt me? I mean, who did he think he was. Of course I forgave him. And I felt quite good about it until my conscience put on a demonstration shouting, "Unfair, hypocrite."

"Whadda ya mean?" I protested. "I forgave the guy, didn't I?"

"Uh-uh," my conscience said. "You just said you did. You only winked at it. You don't know the first thing about forgiveness. Not yet."

"Now wait a minute. When have I refused to forgive anybody?"

"Oh, you haven't refused; you just avoided it. This time you pretended it didn't matter, but that's not what I overheard you tell your wife. And did you forgive that woman last week? You're still brooding over a measly little criticism. And last month—"

"OK, OK, I give in—but if that wasn't forgiving, what is forgiveness?"

"Well," my conscience answered, "it certainly is not tolerance; it's not make-believe; it's not your little game of winking at hurts. It's something much, much deeper."

Losing that argument with my conscience forced me to face one of the most important questions in life. What *is* forgiveness? Does it involve only the little things that are easily forgotten or only the big ones that bruise and ache?

Forgiveness is rare.

"I doubt that very many people actually forgive," a counselee once said to me, "their memory just becomes fatigued. There's a big difference between real forgiveness and a tired memory."

It seems much easier to hold the pain as long as we get reward from reviewing it, and then in exhaustion to dismiss it into the memory hole. No wonder it is rare.

Forgiveness is rare because it is difficult.

Our ideas of justice pull the other way. "He has wronged me; let him pay," we say. "She has done the unforgivable; accepting her is hard."

When a betrayed trust or a fractured friendship stings us, we want to hold the grudge close, to defend ourselves to the last word, and to pin the blame where it is due!

But forgiveness confronts the self that demands its "rights." It repudiates open revenge. It refuses even the polite schemes we often use to get the other back.

Instead, it chooses to hurt, to suffer, and that is one of the hardest voluntary choices we can make—to accept undeserved suffering. Suffering we could have avoided, suffering that rightfully belongs to whomever wronged us.

Forgiveness is difficult because it is costly. The cost may require us to risk further hurt by exploring the injured relationship with someone who caused the injury to begin with. The cost may be that we will have to absorb pain without any satisfactory release and restoration. The cost may require us to accept further rejection when the other brushes us off, blames us further, burns us with additional anger, or blatantly refuses to talk.

So often there is no way to open the conversation of reconciliation. Western society has become so exaggeratedly individualistic that forgiveness has become superficial. It is tolerance or indifference to others. In such a failure of relationship it is tempting to call our forgiving attitude "forgiveness" and go on. Yet the relationship still lies broken.

If we take Jesus' concern for forgiveness as going to the brother or regaining the sister, then we will not reduce forgiveness to an attitude instead of an action. Where the actions of reconciliation are not possible, we feel the failure of the relationship, but we do not excuse it by calling it forgiveness. Often the most we can do is to invite the other to conversation. I must respect their right to refuse to converse. Perhaps they feel overpowered. The power differential between persons can make resolution difficult or even very problematic. Perhaps there are reasons from long past that make this resolution more painful than the person can bear at this time. I will honor their "no" and feel the failure, whatever their reason may be. I will feel the failure of the relationship and remain open for real forgiveness to happen sometime in the future.

In reaching for restored relationship, I must recognize that the new relationship will be different. Often it will be deeper and more rich because we have now met at a deeper level than before. Or we may renegotiate the relationship to a less intimate level that is more appropriate to our needs. When a marriage is ruptured, forgiveness may mean the restoration of the marriage; or it may mean the renegotiation of mutual respect at the level of friendship or shared parenting as single parents. But the anger can be resolved, the pain faced and released, and the relationship resumed at an accountable level.

We must learn to forgive, not to simply overlook or tolerate but to forgive.

We must learn to forgive, not to stop at restoring attitudes of love but to go on to rebuild the broken trust.

We must learn to forgive, not for our private release but for the restoration of relationship and the renewal of community.

We must learn to forgive, seventy times seven.

5

FORGIVENESS AND ANGER

"Sure, I'll forgive that man, when I'm good and ready," the wife says as we sit around the kitchen table.

The forgotten teakettle whistles a forlorn note from the old wood range. The man in question sits, eyes downcast, speechless before her anger.

"If you only knew the misery he's caused me, you'd understand why I'm not going to knuckle in when he says, 'Sorry,'" she continues. "Sure, I'll forgive him, but not until he's paid for a bit of the dirt he's dragged us through."

He steals a glance at her, and the air, hanging heavy with hostility, oppresses like high humidity. We sit in silence. I can see by the set of her jaw that she is reliving one of the many scenes of conflict that happened in this kitchen.

Or is she recalling the day last week when she and her daughter drove into town to confront the woman—"the other woman," as the pulp magazines always put it.

They rang the doorbell and waited. Then the woman stood framed in the screen door, squinting at the daylight, slowly recognizing her callers. Her knuckles glinted white on doorknob. Her face was an impassive mask. They stood mute in mutual hate.

Then the daughter broke it. "I've wanted to see your face for years," she said, "and now that I've seen it," she continued, and spit on the ground, "you make me sick."

"Oh, no, I'm not knuckling under," the wife says again as she gets up from the table. "He can come crawling on his knees for a change."

I'm remembering this scene years later. In the years that passed, the other woman married and moved out of his world. Slowly, bitterly he paid, repaid, and overpaid for all he'd done. At last, one night when she herself was deep in trouble, lonely and desperate, she offered her forgiveness. Too late.

"You can keep your phony forgiving," he told her. "I don't need any of it now. I've paid through the nose for what I did. Who needs forgiveness when he's already paid?"

Central to the work of forgiveness is the task of working through our feelings of anger. In the painful story just told, the anger of the man who betrays his wife, the rage of the woman betrayed, the hostility of the disillusioned daughter, the alienation in "the other woman," the malice of years spent spiting each other, the bitterness of exacting repayment, the wrath of a man long ignored all show how anger takes many forms in human tragedies.

VARIETIES OF ANGER

There is a rich range of anger emotions. To describe them in color one can see a whole spectrum. Red anger is an immediate flash of healthy temper; purple anger is congested, inhibited, internalized; blue anger is becoming depressive and despairing; black wrath has turned toward destructive goals; and white rage sees nothing but its own cold calculating desire for the annihilation of the other. Few of us allow ourselves to feel more than the red anger without quickly denying what we feel and avoiding what we really long to say or do.

Or anger may be described as a range of temperatures.

At the bottom of the thermometer is the icy cold, irrational hostility of frozen hate. Going up, the cool antagonism of continued animosity and long-held grudges.

Then at more normal temperatures, common ordinary touchiness, irritability. You recognize its symptoms—raw sensitivity, impatience at the least difficulty, instant sharp words.

From here on, the mercury soars. There are hot flashes of temper that flare out like bursts of steam. These can turn to boiling, scalding anger—the blood rises, neck and face redden, and the ego will not allow anyone butting in. And the thermometer pops its top when anger explodes into physical violence, which is the high point of anger, lashing out in assault, abuse, and even murder.

With such a spread from the frigidity of hate to the fever of rage, the emotion of anger should be one of our best understood, most carefully managed, and most effectively channeled emotions. It is much too powerful to be overlooked, much too dangerous to be ignored.

Yet it is one of our least understood emotions—our most misunderstood motivation.

Which situations arouse anger for you?

The jealousy when a guy you don't like lands the big job you wanted? Or the resentment when you goof and the other guys rub it in? (Nine out of ten cases of anger are aroused when someone pricks our self-conceit.)

Or the insult when somebody criticizes or pokes fun at your business ability, intelligence, manners, or taste?

It can be the blind anger one feels when a job goes wrong, when things break down, or work piles up.

It may be the frustration you feel when you just can't handle a situation or feel inadequate to perform some needed task.

Obviously, in all these situations, the root cause is the same. The anger springs from some frustration. Anger is the emotion that accompanies demands.

Inside every feeling of anger there are demands. These may be demands for justice and deserve expression, or they may be exaggerated demands and deserve to be canceled.

There are unselfish reasons for anger—anger when another is misused or abused, or anger over an injustice done you. This is valid anger with just demands. And there is self-absorbed, self-centered anger that is concerned only with the self and its narcissistic demands.

Anger as an emotion can be either good or bad, helpful or harmful. It is totally dependent upon the reasons for the anger and how it is exercised.

Anger as an explosion is usually an unnecessary evil, hurtful to you and others. Such anger may be a violent desire to punish others, to inflict suffering, or exact revenge. But anger as an emotion is a morally neutral source of human energy, arousal, and excitement.

If anger can be either right or wrong, how can you judge it when it's possessing you? Do you simply reject all anger out of hand, lumping it all under the uncomplimentary title of sin? Is anger a vice, or is it sometimes a virtue?

From the way most of us act when angry, you might get the impression that anger is shameful. Most people would rather lie than admit they were angry, as though anger were the king of evils, the vice-chairman.

"I was not mad," they say. "Of course I'm not angry."

Or they'll deny it in mid-sentence like the man I overheard yelling, "I am not raising my voice!"

CREATIVE ANGER

Anger can be harmful to us—physically, medically, emotionally, and socially. But it can help, too—in reforming a person, in driving her to shake off slaveries, to attempt new goals and make something of herself.

Anger can be harmful to others in striking out at their personalities, hurting their self-esteem, damaging their emotional balance. But anger can be a great service to others, too. It can challenge injustices or right wrongs that are oppressing others. It can blaze out with a pure force against evil.

The potent anger of an Abraham Lincoln who, seeing the slave market at New Orleans for the first time, reportedly said, "Let's get out of here, boys. If I ever get any chance to hit this thing, I'll hit it hard."

Consider the blazing anger of a Tolstoy against war, of a Gandhi against oppression, of a Martin Luther King against injustice.

Anger disciplined is dynamic, potent. And there is a place for such anger in life. When we no longer feel deeply, even heatedly about right and justice, when "anything goes," when everything is tolerated, all is lost.

Disciplined anger has focused its demands on what is just, on what is the good. It is disciplined because it discards the secondary demands for personal safety and security in order to press for those values that endure.

Gandhi, the great Indian leader and teacher of nonviolence, had this motto on his wall at Sevagram:

> When you are in the right,
> You can afford to keep your temper;
> When you are in the wrong,
> You cannot afford to lose it.

Seneca, the ancient Greek philosopher, wrote, "He is a fool who cannot get angry, but he is a wise man who will not!"

You can use anger or let it use you. If you use anger rightly, it will give your life stamina with its motivation to work for justice, its determination to act with principle and conviction. But if you allow anger to use and abuse you, it can warp and twist your life and mental health.

The question is not, Is anger right or wrong? but, Am I angry about the right things, for the right reasons, and in the right way?

L. E. Maxwell has written: "We have not only the right to be angry, but, at certain situations, we cannot be right unless we are angry, if angry rightly."

A. Powell Davies writes:

> That is one of the truly serious things that has happened to the multitude of so-called ordinary people. They have forgotten how to be indignant. This is not because they are overflowing with human kindness, but because they are morally soft and compliant. When they see evil and injustice, they are pained but

not revolted. They mutter and mumble; they never cry out. They commit the sin of not being angry.

Yet their anger is the one thing above all others that would make them count. If they cannot lead crusades or initiate reforms, they can at least create the conditions in which crusades can be effectual and reforms successful. The wrath of the multitude could bring back decency and integrity into public life; it could frighten the corrupt demagogue into silence and blast the rumormonger into oblivion. It could give honest leaders a chance to win.[1]

PURPOSEFUL ANGER

Christ knew and exercised the emotion of anger. For example, when legalistic, uncaring spectators stood poised like vultures to criticize Christ's free service to others, He showed His anger at their rigid, unfeeling slavery to unjust traditions.

> Then he said to them, "Is it right to do good on the Sabbath day, or to do harm? Is it right to save life or to kill?" There was a dead silence. Then Jesus, deeply hurt as he sensed their inhumanity, looked round in anger at the faces surrounding him, and said to the man, "Stretch out your hand!" And he stretched it out, and the hand was restored as sound as the other one. (Mark 3:4-5)

His anger was over principles of right and wrong, not over persons and personalities. It was not motivated by personal abuse. Calvary called forth the word of forgiving love. But wrong done to others, the abuse of the weak and helpless, ignited His indignation.

1. A. Powell Davies, *The Temptation to Be Good* (Boston: Beacon, 1965), p. 119.

"It were better for [a man] that a millstone were hanged about his neck, and he cast into the sea, than that he should offend one of these little ones" (Luke 17:2, KJV).

Christ's anger was selfless; it was the anger of love. Anger and love are compatible; in fact, a love that is without anger is as worthless as anger that is without love.

CHANNELING ANGER

"Be ye angry and sin not," says the Bible.

> If you are angry, be sure that it is not out of wounded pride or bad temper. Never go to bed angry—don't give the devil that sort of foothold. . . . Let there be no more resentment, no more anger or temper, no more violent self-assertiveness, no more slander and no more malicious remarks. Be kind to one another; be understanding. Be as ready to forgive others as God for Christ's sake has forgiven you. (Ephesians 4:26-27, 31-32)

"Be angry—but beware." You are never more vulnerable to evil than when angry. In anger, self-control is hard put to protect you. Common sense works better at low temperatures. Reason decreases as your emotions rise.

"Be angry, but be aware." Anger soon soars to resentment; it quickly turns bitter. It can lead to temper, hatred, and malice.

"Be angry, but be caring," the Bible concludes. The anger that is motivated by love of your brother, love of the right, and love of God is worthy; it is worth the risk. Its demands are focused on justice, on restoring relationship, and on opening communication.

Self-reflection usually uncovers anger that is also embarrassingly unworthy. Recognizing that fact, learn the virtue of caution. When angry, examine your anger carefully. Don't give it the shadow of the doubt. The Bible suggests such clear self-exploration.

> But what about the feuds and struggles that exist among you—where do you suppose they come from? Can't you see that they arise from conflicting passions within yourselves? You crave for something and don't get it; you are murderously jealous of what others have got and which you can't possess yourselves; you struggle and fight with one another. (James 4:1-2)

In anger, one gets a rare chance to see the self sharply, unretouched. Look and learn. Your anger may be an index to your degree of self-love and self-conceit. Or it may be an unconscious admission of guilt. Guilt that needs to be confessed, forgiven, released. For example, anger is common to those with bad consciences or repressed guilt. A thief is far more angry to be accused of theft than is an honest man. It's more often the adulterer than the faithful spouse who flies into a rage when an affair is revealed. Anger can be far more revealing than even your conscience's warning signals.

When you feel anger mounting, ask, What is my demand? How am I demanding change? What do I really want? An honest answer is like a dash of cold water.

And as a safeguard, check up on the anger that pleases you. It may be the jealousy, envy, or hatred in you that preens itself with fulfillment whenever you humiliate the person who triggers these emotions. It's your pride that delights in the satisfaction of putting down the person who made you lose face.

Nothing feels quite as good as anger when you "just know" you are right and the other deserves the suffering you are about to inflict with self-righteous justice. When you begin to warm up to anger with enjoyment, ask, Why? If you can't find the answer, if your inner feelings of hostility are inexplainable, or if you find yourself constantly irritated, negative in outlook, critical and hostile, then, by all means, get help.

Leon Saul, psychiatrist and author, writes, "I believe man's hostility to man is the central problem in human affairs . . . that it is a disease to be cured and prevented like cancer, tuberculosis, or small pox, and that its cure will result in healthier, better living—not only for society in general but for each individual in particular."[2]

Hostility is an illness when it is always just under the surface, easily aroused, and constantly making a person irritable, touchy, critical, scapegoating, or angry with an impotent rage that's fueled by everything and flares up over nothing. It's an illness when anger is used to accomplish childish goals or to bulldoze through normal conflicts where cooperation, compromise, and understanding should be enough to solve the problem.

Chronic inner hostility is a disease. A disease that results from unwholesome pressures that warp a person's thinking and emotions. Inner anxieties, blocks, frustrations, and guilt feelings can cause hostility to smolder unconsciously in your soul.

In a parlor car on one of the major railways, a man with only a coach ticket wandered in and took someone else's seat, innocently unaware of the small mistake.

The trainman checking tickets mercilessly bawled him out. As the man left the car, another passenger

2. Leon J. Saul, *The Hostile Mind* (New York: Random, 1956), p. 14.

asked him hotly, "Say, why didn't you poke that conductor in the nose? Or at least report him to his superiors?"

"Oh, no," replied the gentleman. "If a man like that can stand himself all his life, surely I can stand him for two minutes."

A good definition of temper is "a method of punishing ourselves for other people's sins."

Repressed anger hurts and keeps on hurting. If you always deal with it simply by holding it firmly in check or sweeping it under the rug, without any form of release or healing, it can produce rigidity and coldness in personality.

Even worse, hostilities pushed down into the depths of consciousness have a way of fermenting into other problems—depression, anxiety, and eventually mental breakdown.

Or repressed anger may come out indirectly in critical attitudes, scapegoating, or irritableness. Often those we call "good people" who harbor hostility will do indirectly and unconsciously what "bad people" do directly and deliberately, because unreleased, buried anger colors their motives.

Repression is an unwholesome and potentially dangerous way of dealing with anger, but obviously it's safer than venting our anger on everybody else.

If the choice is between expressing anger by venting our venom or repressing it, then we better choose the latter. It's safer for others, for society, and ultimately for ourselves.

But there is a third way. It is not expressing or repressing but confessing your anger. Anger and hostility must be released. Somehow you've got to get it off your chest and out of your system. You can either blow it out in steam—or talk it out in honest self-understanding.

Dr. Willard Harris of Ohio State University reports that anger and fear affect the heart in identical ways: the pulse speeds up, and the breathing rate doubles. "Acute anger has been associated with an acute heart attack. Heart damage can be done by repeated bouts of anger over a long period of time."

But more serious is the sickness a hair-trigger temper produces in an explosive personality. It prevents personal and social development, halts spiritual progress, cuts one off from fellow humans, and blocks good judgment.

Temper is a sign of weakness, not strength. Quick temper is an infantile reaction carried over from childhood. Most people never outgrow it completely; some don't even try.

Washington Irving, the early American writer, once noted: "A tart temper never mellows with age, and a sharp tongue is the only edged tool that grows keener with constant use."

When it comes to anger, we're not all created equal. Tempers vary widely. It may be that one person will control as much temper in a given hour as another in a lifetime. If we remember that good spirits are much easier for some than others, we will be a bit less critical.

What a difference in temperaments among Christ's closest friends! Take the contrast of Peter and John, for instance. It may have taken as much grace to keep the apostle Peter from knocking someone down on the street as it took to make John look like an angel of love!

RELEASING ANGER

Release from anger comes from owning up and opening up.

Own up to your anger. Own up to yourself, to those whom you've hurt by your hostility, and own up to God. *Yes*, He already knows all about you, but confessing it to Him is the first step to strength.

The Bible says, "You should get into the habit of admitting your sins to one another, and praying for one another, so that . . . you may be healed" (James 5:16).

When you own up to anger, don't do it just as a grudging admission—*open up*. That is the real test of honest confessing.

You see, the problems of anger and hostility are much deeper than our surface admissions of guilt.

Each of us harbors depths of anger that lie closed and hidden until a moment of stress when the smoldering embers burst into flame. None of us knows how much anger is within us until we are aroused.

George Duncan, the great Scottish Bible teacher, has written: "We never forget anything. In the depths of our minds there is a fearful accumulation of every thought, every emotion we have ever known. *The importance lies in what accumulates*. These depths of human personality need cleansing. The danger is that we deal only with the surface of our lives—like washing our hands and our faces, and thinking we are clean."

The deeper reserves of anger-infection need cleansing if we are to be at peace with ourselves and with others.

You can spend all your life swatting the flies of temper, anger, and irritableness. But far better, clean out the breeding ground down in the depths of your personality.

Honest openness before God and your understanding sister or brother can let the light into your life to begin the healing in depth that God can bring—the healing of forgiveness.

James the apostle writes: "Let every man be quick to listen but slow to use his tongue, and slow to lose his temper. For man's temper is never the means of achieving God's true goodness" (James 1:19-20).

He was quoting that ancient book of wisdom in the Bible, called Proverbs, which has this to say of temper:

> He that is soon angry dealeth foolishly. . . . He that is slow to wrath is of great understanding. . . . He that is slow to anger is better than the mighty; and he that ruleth his spirit than he that taketh a city. . . . The discretion of a man deferreth his anger; and it is his glory to pass over a transgression. (Proverbs 14:17, 29; 16:32; 19:11, KJV)

1. *To channel your anger, slow down.* Learn to delay your anger. Set a later time to settle your conflict or misunderstanding. This is one of the few good uses of the habit of postponing. Put it off till later. Then your emotions will cool off, your head will clear, and your judgment will return.

2. *Don't put it off too long.* Set strict limits on the delay. Don't let yourself do a long, slow burn over anything. Getting mad may be sometimes necessary, but remaining mad never is! So don't store up unfinished anger agenda.

Keep close tab on yourself. Balance all your books by the end of the day. "Don't let the sun go down upon your wrath," the Bible wisely exhorts. The poison of hostility is bad enough in your conscious mind; don't force it down into your subconscious by sleeping on it. Keep up-to-date accounts.

3. *Learn to be honestly open with your anger problem.* Go to the person with whom you were angry. Straighten it out. Life is too short to be ruined with bitter grudges and continuing indignation. Learn to go and make things right—humbly and graciously!

One of the best ways of controlling anger is to talk the problem out with a friend or even yourself. Talking to the mirror, keeping a journal, facing yourself in your own favorite way is indispensable.

Dr. William Menninger counsels: "Do not talk when angry. But after you have calmed down, do talk. Sometimes we push each other away and the problem between us festers and festers. Just as in surgery, free and adequate drainage is essential if healing is to take place."[3]

4. *Examine each anger situation.* Ask yourself, *Exactly why did this touch off my temper?* Self-understanding is a key to anger prevention. Do your best to be understanding of the other person, too. And be sure you understand the true situation between you. It's seldom what it seems to be. All these may help you defuse the explosives in your personality.

The help of an understanding, loving counselor may open the insights you need. A doctor may help you understand how and why these feelings have risen. A minister can guide you in accepting God's forgiveness for your guilt as you receive Jesus Christ as your personal Savior. Then you can accept yourself and go on to full forgiveness of others. You can discover the resources of love that God offers for transforming your

3. William C. Menninger, "Behind Many Flaws of Society," *National Observer* (31 August 1964): 18.

life and for becoming a transformer in the world about you.

Making peace with your own anger and being at peace with another's right to be angry are two qualities that free us to be effective reconcilers. Since forgiveness is, at its heart, the resolution of anger within and between people, it is the person whose anger is accepted, channeled, and directed appropriately who can make peace—seventy times seven.

6

FORGIVENESS AND CONFESSION

"I can't tell her; it would end our relationship," the man said to me, fingering the moisture from his eyebrow. "Under no conditions will I tell my wife. She'd never forgive me, and, well, that's just the way it is. She can't even overlook a little thing like, well, you name it. Just let me slip up on any little thing, and she'll bring up the date and time of day for every other time I did it. No, I can't tell her. She'd lose her temper, slap me once, and then I'd lose my head and—no, I can't."

"Can you live with the memory of your dishonesty, or must you tell her to find relief?" I asked.

"I thought I'd have to tell her all about it to find forgiveness."

"Perhaps that depends on you. If you can accept God's forgiveness and trust Him with your guilt feelings, maybe you won't need to open it up with her to get relief."

"That's what I need, relief," he said. "Only if I confess the mess to her, we'll have a fight that'll end everything that's left between us and tear our kids' hearts out too."

"Couldn't you just leave it right here then—with God? The whole point of confession is to bring healing. To you and to those you've sinned against. If you're sure that it would only be destructive, then go on without it until you feel if that time comes—that you can confess."

"All right, I will," he said. "But what if she finds out about it?"

"In that case, I'll stand by you and assure her that you made an honest break and were truly repentant."

"One thing you can be sure of, it's good-bye deceit from now on."

He reached for his hat and was gone. Hopefully leaving behind his guilt with the bitter story.

A story of marriage and marriage conflicts, of finances and financial struggles, of status and status scrambles. The story of a thousand families torn apart by the new house, new decor, new car, new securities, and the race for new trophies and new triumphs. Tragedy enough in itself, but laced with the private tragedies of twisted lives.

Two careers, two schedules, two independent businesses developed into two mutually exclusive lives, except for those rare times when they found themselves making conversation and fabricating a fragile front of happiness for the sake of the three children.

Then success began to break in the wife's business. Regional administration fell into her lap. Money began flowing more freely. Two-day absences grew into four-day conventions.

Fortunately for her, a friend with nothing to do loved to come in, care for the kids, and fix a little food for the husband. But all too soon proximity, availability, mutual loneliness, and the chemistry of evenings under the same roof did their work. The friendly chats turned into intimacy. Duplicity matured into infidelity as weeks multiplied into months of betrayal.

Then the youngest child caught rheumatic fever. The wife, finally feeling motherly concern, dropped her work to nurse the child back toward health.

Then all the tensions between them began to twist beneath the surface. With both women sometimes around the house, he fled it in fear.

He plunged himself deeper into his work, but nothing silenced the nagging whisper of guilt, the fear that she would find him out and that the scandal would ruin his career, his reputation, his home and life.

At last he turned to someone to talk it out, insisting, "I've got to get relief, but if it can only come by confessing, then I'll forget it." Gradually he opened himself to God. Now, *now* what would he do?

The next day he was back, and I knew immediately from his face that he had told her, and yet somehow everything was all right.

"It was after dinner," he said, "when she asked me point blank, 'What is it about you tonight? You're like you haven't been for years.' What was I to say? I was, well, speechless. And before I knew what I was doing, I blurted it out. I told her. Told her what I'd done to her and to the kids. Told her it'd all happened between me and her best friend.

"She sat, head in hands, until it was all out. Then she asked, 'Is it really true?' 'Yes,' I said. 'And is that all?' 'Yes.' The silence flowed by.

"Then she stood, stepped over behind me, and touched my hair. I looked up to see her eyes all tear-shiney.

" 'I forgive you,' she said. 'Let's start over from here; let's go on with life together.'

"It was too much for me to take. Then—then I saw that I was trembling; my teeth clicked for a moment before I caught them; everything blurred.

" 'Why,' she said in surprise, 'why, you're angry.' I nodded my admission. 'You wanted me to hit you, didn't you?' Slowly I admitted the truth.

" 'No,' she said, 'I wouldn't hit you; that would only have justified everything you did. And it might have touched off both our tempers for the last time. No, no, I forgive you. That's our only hope if we're ever going to live again.'

"That's when healing happened," the man told me. "Her forgiving me like that, it, well, it broke my heart, or it broke down my last resistance, my last self-justification. You see, I was still blaming her and her work and busy schedule for my unfaithfulness. And her forgiveness was so unexpected, it was like she reached into resources I didn't know she had and forgave me. She gave me back my life."

Could he have really found forgiveness without confession? Certainly he had to confess it to someone. To a friend who would be understanding and help him face his problem in honesty; to God, the only true source of forgiveness and release.

But to his wife? That's the crux of a very difficult problem. Yes, the sin of adultery was committed against her. Yes, it needed to be made right. But that's first repentance, secondarily confession.

If the man repents, that is, honestly and completely turns away from his past and its sins, must he confess it all? Certainly confession will bring a tremendous release and relief for his tortured feelings of guilt. But what then? Will she be able to forgive, forget, and accept him again? Will the confession be constructive, bringing healing and health once more to their relationship? Or will it be a block that nothing will be able to remove for her? Will it embed hostilities in her soul that she is not emotionally, spiritually, and mentally able to overcome? Will it be constructive or destructive of love, understanding, and acceptance?

Then when and where should confession be made?

Confession should be as public as the commission of the act. Only those directly involved should be told in your confession. Sin should not be published for general public consumption and speculation.

Confession should be shared where it is a help to another, not a hurt or a hindrance. If confessing your sin would provide another with excuses or tempt another to stumble, don't!

Confession should not be so intimate, so revealing, so painful that it will wound or scar the person to whom it is confessed. Such careless, thoughtless confession to a close friend or lover may bring you release, but it will transfer the painful burden to the other. One person is healed at the expense of another. It is rarely wise to confess by "telling all," down to the small details, to your most intimate friends. Go first to a Christian friend who cares but would not be personally harmed. Any brother or sister who knows how to live openly in the light can hear your confession and help you find release.

If you should choose not to confess, for the sake of being redemptive and loving to the other person, be aware that you are choosing the harder, not the easier way. To live with the unspoken memory of your sin, to find forgiveness without sharing the meaning of that forgiveness, is not an easier way. It is all the more demanding of you and your own spiritual and emotional maturity. This is true, because essentially, confession is a human necessity.

We discover and experience release from our guilt in direct proportion to our willingness to face our sin, confess our sinfulness, and accept forgiveness.

GUILT AS A GIFT

Guilt is a much maligned emotion. This comes as no surprise to anyone, since the pain that guilt causes is one of the earliest sources of intense inner discomfort. Yet guilt is not only necessary for healthful living, it is a gift to be used wisely as well as a burden to be lifted.

For most of us, the capacity to feel guilt is something to be prized; the content of our guilt deserves to be explored, expressed, and released. The guilt accumulation within may reach back to our third and fourth years when the first guilt feelings began to emerge from our early childhood sense of shame.

Guilt reserves slowly accumulate from the frustrations caused by parents who shouted, "No, no, no," by brothers and sisters who chanted, "Naughty, naughty, naughty," and by teachers who demanded, "Now aren't you ashamed of yourself? You shouldn't have done that." Much of this collected guilt is constructed from false fears that should be forgotten. But within this storehouse of guilt feelings there is authentic guilt, which is a necessary process of inner direction.

Guilt is both true and false. There is true guilt, which must be faced and forgiven. And there is false guilt, which may be faced and forgotten.

Guilt is a sense of wrongdoing, an emotional conflict that arises out of second thoughts on something we have done. If we have violated our accepted moral or social standards, or even if we imagine we have violated them, an accusing voice within us cries, "Guilty!"

And for many the repeated accusations of a tortured conscience haunt life with a never sleeping specter of remorse and regret, ruining happiness and spoiling possibilities.

Guilt, with all its complexities, is a terrifying foe for anyone. Trying to identify it is somewhat like wrestling an octopus in a darkened aquarium at midnight.

For most of us, guilt exists on three levels.

The main floor of this three-storied guilt is the area of normal experience and interchange with people. Here, in the court of social opinion, we become aware of our guilt before others.

Our first feelings of guilt do come from others. They are born in a child's mind when parents scold. They spring from the fear that a parent's love may turn to hostility.

All through our maturing years, our fear of the taboos of our family and friends gives birth to guilt feelings. These vary, of course, according to the moral and social standards that are found in our society.

An African bush mother might feel guilty if she does not throw a set of identical twins to the jackals. Yet in our communities such a mother would be guilty of murder.

But in all societies, when a member falls short of the requirements of life with others, he or she loses face on the outside and feels guilty inside.

Guilt before others, or "social guilt," arises whenever a person's actions are blameworthy in the social environment. Such guilt may be true or false, depending on the taboo involved.

The second floor of guilt is the guilt of our feelings. Let's consider the experiences we might encounter in the court of the mind (or often the imagination).

GUILT BEFORE SELF

Self can be a most lenient judge, or it can be mercilessly cruel. Some individuals are capable of mastering their feelings and thus leading a healthy emotional life. Their feelings of guilt are dealt with promptly, clearly, and forthrightly.

But others depress themselves by elaborating on their blameworthiness. They build vast air castles of fantastic guilt feelings reaching many stories into the sky.

These imaginary skyscrapers of neurotic guilt usually divert everyone's attention from the real problem of guilt, festering deep within the soul.

Fantastic guilt feelings can be a camouflage for our true guilt.

Why? Because it is in the basement story down in the depths of our being that we find the foundation of all true guilt.

GUILT BEFORE GOD

This is not just a guilt we face in the court of our minds or in the court of public opinion. This is guilt that summons us all before the judgment seat of God.

This is true guilt, because you and I are guilty before God. We—all of us—are "sinners" (certainly no one can argue long about that). We have all sinned and fallen short (Romans 3:23).

We are at one and the same time free to sin and bound to sin! We are not sinners because we sin; we sin because we are sinners.

Our guilt before God is not contained or defined by any specific incident, yet it is there, behind every act and thought of evil. It is the great underlying stratum, the foundation structure of all true guilt. We are not what we ought to be, and we know it! We feel it. And we fear it.

In the clear light of the rightness and wholeness of God, every mouth is stopped and all the world stands guilty before God (Romans 3:19).

You and I are truly guilty here, deep down in our personalities. Down where we are helpless to remold our lives; we wouldn't even know where to begin!

Now, about your feelings of guilt and how you can discover if they are true or if they are false: Since all true guilt is guilt before God, then the only valid measuring stick for your feelings is the Word of God!

"The Bible illuminates our problem in a remarkable way," says Swiss physician Paul Tournier in his book *Guilt and Grace.* "From now on, 'false guilt' is that which comes as a result of the judgments and suggestions of men. 'True guilt' is that which results from divine judgment."

As you govern your life honestly by the Word of God and deal openly with the problems of true guilt in your life, you will free yourself from the false guilts suggested and assigned to you by people and by the pressures of friends and foes.

False guilt is dangerous, but true guilt is deadly. It gnaws at the heart, weakens character, sours the disposition, and works its own punishment.

Guilt can be deadly, if it is covered and kept. But guilt is meant to be a help, not a hurt! Repressed guilt is destructive, but confessed guilt is redemptive! Guilt that works renewal in our lives is a gift worthy of our gratitude! Guilt is an inner alarm system that was not made to be ignored but to be obeyed!

Guilt is a goad to prod us toward repentance and forgiveness. Guilt should move us toward regret and perhaps remorse. And remorse is only a step away from repentance.

Now, remorse is good, as far as it goes, but it stops short of giving release. An honest sense of guilt usually brings sorrow. But sorrow needs to change into positive action, or else it spirals in on itself—swells into greater and greater remorse, even to suicide. Sorrow and remorse are only meant to be the first steps toward repentance, toward a change of heart.

Paul the apostle praised his Christian friends at Corinth because their sorrow led to repentance and release. Listen to his words: "The result was to make you sorry as God would have had you sorry. . . . The sorrow which God uses means a change of heart and leads to salvation—it is the world's sorrow that is such a deadly thing" (2 Corinthians 7:9-10).

Sorrow can be deadly? Sorrow sours quickly into the bitter misery of blind regret. Oh, if it never had happened! But what can we do? Roll back the clock? Undo the deeds? Impossible! Remorse repeats its routine of regrets and reprisals. If a guilty person never gets beyond this point, sorrow does more harm than good. It turns into anger at being caught, fear of being found out, or frustration that others "got away with it."

It doesn't need to turn out that way. "The sorrow which God uses means a change of heart." That's repentance. A change of mind and heart. It is necessary for release of guilt; more, it is the basis of right relations with God.

In repentance, the heart is not only broken for its sins, it is broken from its sins as well. Mere sorrow, which sits and weeps out its regret, is not repentance. Repentance is sorrow converted into action. Right actions in the future are the only true apologies for wrong actions in the past. To claim repentance without revolution of life is like continually bailing a swamping boat but never plugging the leak.

"To do so no more is the truest repentance," wrote Martin Luther.

It is a change of direction—"Turn to God." Some people believe it's only a mental matter, but to spin on your heel and turn to follow God requires a complete change in purpose and in pursuits. Remorse will cause a person to halt repeatedly but then continue in the same path. Repentance is an about-face.

Jesus considered repentance as indispensable. "Unless you repent, you too will all perish" (Luke 13:5, NIV). And speaking even to the "good people" of His day, Jesus said, "Thieves, tax collectors and prostitutes will enter heaven before you because you will not repent and believe" (paraphrase; see Matthew 21:31-32).

And there are the two sides to repentance. It is a turning from sin and a turning to God in believing faith.

Where do we begin?

FACE IT

To face your sin is to discover openness. This is release that comes from simply taking inventory of your life and finding the courage to do something about your guilt feelings or any known sin that you have harbored. The courage to face sin leads to the next step.

CONFESS IT

To confess your sin is to discover honesty. Not that it's new, but it's rare. Release comes through confession of sin to the one wronged, to the Christian friend who is standing by you with his love and concern, or even to a group of people—if they are the ones you have involved.

The decision to confess sin sets in motion a course of action.

FORSAKE IT

To forsake your sin is repentance! Release demands the willingness to say good-bye to the old burdens of guilt and sin, and that, of course, means forsaking the cause of it all.

When you have surrendered your guilt, accepting forgiveness, then you will want to take one more step for your new life.

LIVE IT

Live forgiveness! Go on to enjoy to the full living in a new released way! You will discover that your greatest weakness can become your greatest strength through the transforming power of God.

To summarize what we have explored, we have stressed that confession can free one from the past and commit one to a new future.

True confession has two sides. Confession with only a negative side is a counterfeit. It's the admit-your-failures-and-get-them-off-your-chest variety. But true confession has a positive side, too. It is a confession of dependence and allegiance to God, the great Guilt-remover.

Let's examine both sides of confession.

CONFESSION OF SINFULNESS

You must own up to your sinfulness. Admit your helplessness, your weakness, your need. Yes, this is the negative side, but it is a necessary side. Guilt wants to stay hidden. It breeds best in isolation. It loves the dark unswept corners of our personalities.

Like a termite, it eats and destroys when hidden, but, when brought to the light, it dries up and dies.

Three thousand years ago, David, king of Israel, described the bone-rot of guilt like this:

> When I kept silent, my bones wasted away through my groaning all day long. For day and night your hand was heavy upon me; my strength was sapped as in the heat of summer. *Selah.* Then I acknowledged my sin to you and did not cover up my iniquity. I said, "I will confess my transgressions to the Lord"—and you forgave the guilt of my sin. (Psalm 32:3-5, NIV)

Such confession is not the shallow "Dear-God-I-goofed-again" sort. It is confession in depth that goes down to the root of sin—down to our sin-prone self. Listen in again on David's confession: "For I know my transgressions, and my sin is always before me. Against you, you only, have I sinned and done what is evil in your sight" (Psalm 51:3-4, NIV).

"When the Bible talks of confession," writes William Klassen, "it never describes a simple mental process, but always an activity that takes place in public. We confess with our lips!"[1]

The Bible says, "Confess your sins to each other and pray for each other" (James 5:16, NIV).

Why must we admit to another? Because only in the humiliation of honest confession can we be freed from our guilt.

When I stand before my sister or brother honestly, as I truly am, when through confession I bring my sin out into the light, then sin dies. My endless circle of

1. William Klassen, *The Forgiving Community* (Philadelphia: Westminster, 1966), p. 45.

self-justification is broken. My defenses fall. My guilt is uncovered; the light reveals it, and it dies.

Why is this so important? Because refusal to confess —that is, to live honestly and openly in the light—is actually walking in darkness, living a lie. To pretend perfection and peace where in reality there is hidden guilt and secret sin is the height of hypocrisy.

But according to the apostle John, "if we confess our sins [notice this is plural; we confess specific concrete sins], he is faithful and just and will forgive us our sins and purify us from all unrighteousness" (1 John 1:9, NIV).

But that's only the negative side of confession. We must take positive action as well.

CONFESSION OF SURRENDER

Surrender is the positive side. To find real release from guilt, you must also confess your faith. A faith in Jesus Christ who removes guilt of all shapes and sizes.

You must confess with your own mouth that Jesus Christ is your Lord, and believe in your heart. For it is by believing in his heart that a man becomes right with God, and with his mouth he confesses his faith (Romans 10:9-10).

A moment of complete honesty, a moment when we come to true confession of who and what we are is an eternal moment of truth. The greatest, clearest moment of truth open to us happens when we see what we should be in Jesus Christ, confess that truth, and commit ourselves to following it.

Such a moment of truth can peel our eyes to life's deepest meaning. And as we confess it, we come face to face with what that truth demands: death to the old way of life.

We must die in order to truly know ourselves and our God. This is not the cold chill of physical death. (Although that would certainly open our eyes to ultimate truth.) Rather, it is an internal death of our selfish will, of our self-centered motives.

In some of his most unforgettable words, the apostle Paul described death to the old self:

> As far as I am concerned, I consider my old self as good as dead, crucified along with my Master, Christ. And my present life is not that of the old "I," but the living Christ within me. The new life I now live, I live by faith in the Son of God who loved me and sacrificed himself for me. (Galatians 2:20, paraphrase)

That is a description of a moment of truth before God that gave Paul a motive for living.

The late A. W. Tozer used to explain this experience of crucifying the self like this: "The man on the cross is facing in only one direction. He is not going back, and he has no further plans of his own."[2]

You trade your old self-centered ambitions for a new ambition—to let God be God in all of your life. With new goals like that, you haven't got anyone to fight, to use, or to climb over.

You trade your old self-centered reputation for a new life-style—one that lets Jesus Christ be seen in your life. With that kind of purpose, you've nothing to be phony or proud about.

You trade in your old self-justifications and pretense to goodness for new peace and forgiveness. God accepts you; you accept yourself and forgive others. With that, you've nothing to be angry and bitter about.

2. A. W. Tozer, "Total Commitment," *Decision* (August 1963): 4.

And since you've died to earth-centered living and are alive to God, no one can kill you!

A moment of truth before the Master can bring you a motive of truth for all of life. Your whole life with its frustrations, regrets, weaknesses, and strengths can become new as Jesus Christ enters and controls your mind and heart. That's how He makes it all new.

He lives in you. That is, He will live in your life when you die to your old self by exclusively rejecting everything you know to be wrong, everything that is opposed to Jesus Christ.

Accept, inclusively, all that Jesus Christ is, does, and gives, and His new life in you will begin.

Then you will come to the greatest of all moments of truth—absolute honesty before Jesus Christ. Pledge your whole self to Him and let Him be truly the Master of your life. That is the crucial confession that leads to forgiveness.

7

FORGIVENESS AND MARRIAGE

"No, I will not forgive you," the husband said.

It had been difficult for her to face him, difficult to ask for forgiveness, difficult to admit what had happened between them.

"I never intended to have an affair," she began, "but my life was so empty. With the children both in school, I needed something to give me meaning. When I went back to college I found another world of friendships. I tried to talk with you about my new circle of associates, but you were so busy. And I was getting farther and farther away from you. When I started going out with Ray, I knew I was wrong, but I was angry at you, and your job, and all the time you spent away. I realize how wrong it was to get even in this way. I am sorry. I hope someday there can be forgiveness."

"I hope so, too," the man replied.

"You do? But you just said—"

"I just said I won't forgive you, and I also said I hope there will be forgiveness between us."

"I don't understand."

"The last thing I want is for me to forgive you, as if I were totally in the right, and you were the sole wrong-doer. No, I'm afraid of what that would do to us both for the rest of our lives. I want to find out what my part was in all this. Maybe then we can forgive each other."

"You do want forgiveness?"

"Yes, but not the kind my sister gave to her husband. He's been paying through the nose ever since. I want to work through whatever it is between us and see if we can't begin again."

Forgiveness in marriage is rarely a one-way matter. It takes two to have a problem; people don't have problems alone. More often responsibility lies somewhere between the partners rather than at either doorstep. People who marry each other are drawn together by similarities too deep for either to recognize. They may be attracted by their surface differences and superficial similarities, but at the core there are profound processes that bond them to one another and blind them to much that is taking place between them.

Forgiveness in marriage must be two-way, or it is not forgiveness at all. Rather it becomes a covert strategy for expressing judgment, perhaps condemnation, that may alienate the two for ever after. Sometimes the most destructive thing one can do in a relationship is to "forgive" the other person. When authentic forgiveness happens, both are changed, both come to meet the other, both pledge to reconstruct the relationship, both seek genuine repentance for whatever has happened.

The righteous anger of the one party must be surrendered along with the the defensive anger of the other. Both share in creating the relationship that allowed, perhaps invited, the hurts that have arisen. Both must journey across the distance that divides them if they are to truly meet. Reconciliation comes when there is mutual openness and mutual willingness to change. This is what the Bible refers to as mutual submission. It is a mutual caring—a mutual concern for the other's welfare.

THE ATMOSPHERE OF FORGIVING

The marriage relationship that welcomes reconciliation of differences, renegotiation of understandings, and reconstructing of relationships has an atmosphere of liberating love. This freedom of forgiveness is something that must be felt to be fully appreciated. Each sets the other free to live spontaneously, to live joyfully and fully, to live with an honest openness and an open honesty.

The normal Western family does not allow such freedom. Most families handle their differences by not talking about them, avoid their conflicts by denying that they exist, and bury their problems under a surface of niceness. (For one who loves honesty and genuineness, life with chronically nice, even terminally nice, people is cloying. At times one prays, "Please God, not one more cheerful person today. Could I have just one who is real?")

This atmosphere of avoidance and denial, maintained out of peace-loving motives, requires a blindness to injustice, a deafness to feelings, an insensitivity to the hurts of relationship. Jesus once described the conspiracy of silence among good people in startling words:

> They seeing, see not. And hearing they hear not, neither do they understand. By hearing ye shall hear and shall not understand; seeing ye shall see and shall not perceive. For the heart waxes gross, the ears dull of hearing, the eyes are closed lest at any

time, they should see with their eyes and hear with their ears, and understand with their heart, and should turn and change and be healed. (Matthew 13:9, 13-16, paraphrase)

The atmosphere of freedom, to both fail and succeed—to be human—is central to love for the other person. If one loves only the successful, appreciates only the beautiful, cares only for another when the other is performing, complying, achieving, then there is no real love at all. Love sets the other free to be human. It cancels conditions and accepts the other without reservations.

There are five freedoms visible in such an atmosphere of marital acceptance and unconditional familial love.

1. *The freedom to see what one sees.* Love sets us free to see what is; the old denial process demands that we live by silent "loyalties" that bind and blind. The more I love you, the more I set you free. The more I feel obligated to "loyalty," the more I must refuse to see what is, deny what was, and avoid what might be. So I rewrite the past, read out threats, read in fantasies. Our life together becomes a charade, a pretense, a mime.

The family that keeps faith sets each person free to see.

2. *The freedom to think one's own thoughts.* Respect invites each person to think one's own thoughts. "Obligations" pressure one to repeat others' ideas without making them one's own, to replicate others' lives without understanding, to be a recorded announcement with an identity that is secondhand.

The family that respects persons invites each person to think.

3. *The freedom to feel one's own feelings.* Caring sets another free to feel, to feel positive and negative emotions, to own irritation and affection. Fear intimidates one to suppress feelings, repress excitement, depress hopes of being fully present with others. So the senses are dulled, feelings are cut off, people become superficial, surface, saintly, and safe.

The family that cares for persons frees them to feel.

4. *The freedom to choose what one wants.* Valuing another is honoring the freedom to respond voluntarily, choose with integrity, will with inner direction, want what one truly wants. Shame coerces one to submit blindly to outer direction, to yield the will in self-doubt, to yield up the privilege of personhood.

The family that values another values voluntary response.

5. *The freedom to act—to speak, to risk, and to be real.* Prizing another is delighting in that person's freedom to act as a responsible being, to speak as a real person of integrity, to risk living as a genuine person working out full fidelity with self, with others, with God. Selflessness leads us to be copies of others, conforming to patterns that are not one's own acts of centered commitment.

The family that prizes each other prizes integrity.

When partners in a marriage are free to see reality, think with honesty, feel with integrity, choose responsibly, and act maturely, they create an atmosphere that invites children to mature fully.

In such family living, perfection is no longer seen as required, but maturity is prized. Conformity is no longer coerced; responsibility is valued. Failure is not feared; forgiveness is practiced.

Since most persons grow up in families that are less than open, genuine, warm, caring, and free in the ways we have been describing, it is the norm for marriages to struggle through repeated times of severe stress. Healthy marriages do not avoid such stressful times; they recognize, welcome, and work through them. They recognize that the passage between one stage of life and the next may be stormy, yet the weathering of the tempest is what gives life depth, and forgiveness the richness that infuses life with grace.

For many couples, accepting the help of others in the Christian community is a great source of support, whether this comes from other couples, from a pastor, or from a person trained in marriage counseling.

Most of us quickly see a dentist when a tooth aches, a mechanic when the car breaks down, or a doctor when pain strikes. Why not get help when marriage gets stormy?

What are the danger signals?

INCREASING DISTANCE

The first danger signal is an increase in distance between two partners. Check to see if you are retreating from your problems instead of resolving them, allowing distance to prevent you from finding forgiveness.

Difficulties in living together are opportunities for growth. Forget the romantic propaganda that insists: "A happy marriage has no conflicts, no problems, no irritating disagreements—there can be no anger."

If such marriages are made in heaven, they must stay there. They rarely appear here on earth.

Any marriage will have problems, because normal growth creates new situations, with new demands that require new understandings. So of course there are conflicts. Misunderstanding is inevitable. Disagreements are unavoidable. Anger is always possible.

A marriage—like every living thing—is in constant danger of deterioration. It also offers the possibility of continuing growth and maturation.

And that's a task for both. There must be a mutual involvement in resolving the tensions and conflicts that arise. Creating an atmosphere of forgiveness and acceptance is primary agenda for Christian marriage.

LOSS OF COMMUNICATION

The second signal is loss of communication. Have you reached the point where you just can't communicate and both freeze into uncomfortable and unyielding silences, broken only by hostile words or ironical digs? Has irritation replaced affection?

To open up communication, the first task is to listen. Listening is 90 percent of good communication. It's not just "the other half of talking." It's a skill—one that must be learned and practiced. All the time. Most people find it hard even to listen half the time, and then only with half of their mind.

Genuine, attentive listening has become so unusual that finding a good listener almost makes you lose your train of thought. Like the wife whose husband dropped his newspaper and turned full attention on her.

"Stop it," she snapped. "You're deliberately listening just to confuse me."

Actually, to listen is the queen of compliments; to ignore, the chief of insults. To become human, everyone needs listeners and, to be human, each must learn to listen.

Do you know how to listen? Or do your eyes stray and betray your wandering interests? (A good listener listens with the eyes, too.)

Do you let others' words and ideas fly by while you plan your next comment, cooking up some sage word with which to stun them at the first opportunity?

Do you interrupt others or, even worse, second-guess them, trying to finish the line, or coach when they stumble for a word?

Do you probe, question, interrogate, cross-examine, thus suggesting impatience or superiority?

Or do you truly listen? Can you go beyond merely hearing words and phrases to catch the ideas? And beyond the ideas, to the feelings? Beyond the expressions to the true intent?

That's listening—with love for others.

Love is a warm listener!

Haven't you experienced it? Have you ever talked with someone who listened with such abandon and attention to what you were trying to say that it drew you out? Called forth your best? Even helped clarify your thoughts by the very quality of listening?

Or have you started out to vent your inner agonies and complain bitterly against your circumstances, but your friend's understanding love given in complete attention made you see things in a new light, and instead of collecting a quart of sweet sympathy you simply unloaded your problem.

Remember when you were involved in a personal tragedy? Did you want someone to talk to you? Give you a speech of sympathy? Or a little sermonette of encouragement? No, you wanted someone who loved you enough to sit down and listen to your feelings, to give understanding and acceptance in spite of your problem.

And some people didn't care enough to listen. Their words didn't matter, even though they did keep up a running patter of "keep-a-stiff-upper-lip, every-cloud-has-a-silver-lining, look-on the-bright-side, after -all-it-might-have-been worse."

I'll never forget a moment of tragedy in my life when I needed help and turned to an old friend to share a bit of my suffering. After three sentences, he interrupted to give me a flawlessly worded, lovely speech. But the farther he went, the more distant it became. I wanted to reach out, grasp his lapel, and say, "Come back. I don't want a bouquet of words. I want you!"

But who am I to criticize? How often I've given a friend in need the stone of eloquent comfort when what was wanted was the bread of human understanding. No matter how polished, perfect, and multifaceted the stone, it offers no nourishment. You can't eat diamonds. Even if they are "forever."

Loving is listening. Caring is hearing.

Love is the opening of your life to another—through sincere interest, simple attention, sensitive listening, compassionate understanding, and honest sharing.

An open ear is the only believable sign of an open heart. You learn to understand life—you learn to live —as you learn to listen.

To love your neighbor is to listen as you listen to yourself. The golden rule of friendship is to listen to others as you would have them listen to you.

Listening—it's the key to true friendship, loyalty, and understanding between any and all persons in all relationships: parent-child, employer-employee, and, most important of all, husband-wife relationships.

Communication begins with listening. It grows with genuine understanding.

For husband and wife, being understanding is the crucial step toward *being* the right mate. Whether or not you found "the right mate" is not the important thing for happiness in marriage. The crucial step is your willingness to *be* the right person to your partner.

In his book *To Understand Each Other*, Paul Tournier points out that "when a husband complains, 'But she doesn't understand me,' or 'I just can't understand that woman,' he is only saying in shorthand, 'I don't think she accepts me,' or 'I can't accept my wife.' But the commitment to be understanding, loving, accepting can begin to change all that."

GROWING RESENTMENT

The third danger signal comes when you let the attitudes or actions of the other irritate, alienate, and fester within you. Then you begin letting them accumulate from day to day. You take them to bed at night, refusing to make up, and you "let the sun go down upon your wrath" (Ephesians 4:26, KJV).

This calls for a real change of tactics. Begin working at dissolving your frustrations with love: by risking increasing levels of openness. Talk over both problems and successes. Don't rely on the other to read your feelings. Don't say, "He knows I'm angry. Why doesn't he apologize?"

After a few years of marriage, nonverbal communication may become pretty common, but it is powerless to solve problems. You've got to discuss and talk it out.

Openness is the channel of love. Love is the opening of your life to another. The trust that lays life bare to another. Such trust is possible where people frequently reaffirm their pledge of faithful loyalty.

True loyalty is a pledge of unconditional allegiance to one another in thoughts, plans, actions, and attitudes. It is a pledge that must be demonstrated in full acceptance of the other in an until-death-do-us-part contract. Loyalty is a matter of priorities. And a husband-wife promise of love is by very nature an exclusive promise that eliminates all competition. He or she comes first and knows it! That assurance of first loyalty is the source of true security.

We all crave the security that comes from belonging to someone who loves us in return for our love. We long for the joy we can feel when we are bringing happiness to someone we love. We need the security that intimacy, open honesty, and acceptance give. And security is possible only where there is fidelity. Unity, loyalty, and security are totally dependent on fidelity to each other.

The late Swiss theologian Emil Brunner once wrote, "Marriage is based not so much on love as on fidelity."

That fidelity is an allegiance of life with no reservation, no hesitation. It is more than fidelity in sexuality. It is being faithful in thought as well as act, faithful in fulfilling the deep emotional and spiritual needs of the other, and faithful in solving or resolving the inevitable misunderstandings and conflicts. Such a marriage is only possible when it is cemented and re-cemented by forgiving love.

The husband and wife who discover the deepest levels of intimacy are those who give each other the completely unconditional acceptance of depth forgiveness. They reach toward total forgiveness knowing that it brings a unity that is truly complementary and complete. In resolving the conflicts that come, happiness will happen. The difficulties of life, rightly met, will draw you together.

"A good difficulty in your marriage can be marvelous," one wife said. "When you accept it as a challenge and resolve it, other things that are pulling you apart fade into the background. You go on loving and forgiving."

In marriage, even more than in all other arenas of life, forgiveness must be seventy times seven.

8

FORGIVENESS AND PREJUDICE

The trial is in its final hours.

After days of prosecution, finally the defense is to be heard. Day after day witnesses have amassed evidence.

Guilty.

At last the case for the defense. But wait! Where is the jury? What! Gone out for coffee? And the judge? He's nodding at his desk! The defense is being presented, but no one is there to hear. No one but you!

And *you* are the defendant. It is your trial. You are on trial for life, without defense. No one will hear your side of the case. No one cares.

Now you realize, now you see through it all. You were judged before the trial even began, sentenced even before the evidence was heard, condemned without mercy, as good as dead before you ever came to court.

What if that were you!

What if you were judged without opportunity of reply and condemned for false reasons mouthed by false witnesses in a false trial?

What if you were prejudged—by others' prejudices? What if it happened to you?

Hasn't it? Doesn't it? Are you not judged without defense by all those who label, stereotype, criticize, or condemn you simply on the basis of their prejudices?

And don't you do it too? Every time you offer a prejudicial statement, make a prejudiced judgment, or laugh at a bit of prejudiced merriment?

Prejudice is prejudging—weighing another man or his viewpoint with your thumb on the scales.

Prejudice is passing a judgment of discrimination against others on the basis of things they did not cause, could not change, and should not regret.

There is nothing logical about it at all. Nothing reasonable, rational, or responsible. Prejudice answers to none of these. It's an emotion, not a conviction.

When we speak of prejudices we say, "I feel." When we speak of opinions we say, "I think." When we speak of convictions we say, "I know!"

You may challenge convictions with logic or change opinions by argument. But not prejudices. They can't be put into words that easily. They are nonverbal reactions that we seldom realize we possess.

Where did they come from, these prejudices of ours?

To begin with, few of us were taught to be prejudiced. We caught it—like a disease. It is an illness—a character disease that is transmitted as easily and accidentally as any physical sickness.

You and I are infected. We are all prejudiced. What's worse, we are carriers. Our children catch it from us as they "catch on" to the hidden meanings of our uncaring words or our unfeeling jokes. Any slip of the tongue, innocent as it may seem, can build unhealthy attitudes or leave a residue of prejudice.

Prejudice is the sour deposit that accumulates in any dent or crevice in your character.

It began accumulating when you were two years old, accelerated in early school years, and, now, who knows what lies hidden in the depths of your mind? You may not be responsible for all the prejudices that rubbed off onto you in your maturing years, but why are you still using them, why are you letting them use you?

There may have been a day when such snobbish feelings of superiority would have been winked at. But that day is past. There is no room in our shrinking world for prejudice. If you think you're superior to any other because your skin is white, or pink, or tan, forget it. Such prejudices have long been disproved, and it's high time they were despised and discarded.

There is a way to find release from your prejudices. There is a way for you, whether you are a Christian in a white, Anglo-Saxon Protestant church, a not-yet-Christian wondering if faith in Christ can make any difference, or an *indeed*-I'm-not-a-Christian pointing out the uncomfortable fact that 11:00 A.M. on Sunday is still the most segregated hour of the week.

Consider the one absolutely unprejudiced Man who ever lived, the one Person who offered personal, social, spiritual, and moral help in conquering prejudice. Jesus Christ!

"Now wait," you may say, "the followers of Christ are among the most prejudiced people in our nation." Yes, some of them are. Harvard psychologist Gordon Allport in his book *The Nature of Prejudice* writes, "The role of religion is paradoxical. It makes prejudice and

it unmakes prejudice . . . . Churchgoers are more prejudiced than the average; they are also less prejudiced
than the average."[1]

Why this polarity, this vast difference? Why does
religion make some people bigoted and intolerant, but
make others more understanding, caring, and accepting?

Could it be that those who use religion—for status,
security, or social opportunity—accept only the parts
of religion that reinforce their own views?

But those who, in faith, commit themselves unre-
servedly to follow Jesus Christ in life find something
else? Can it be that they find a new strength in Christ
to love their neighbor? Or a new pattern in Christ for
what it means to be a human being to fellow humans, a
child of God to all His other children? Can it be that as
they die to prejudice, as Christ promised, they are born
again to a life of love?

Can it be that He can remove the beam of prejudice from their eyes?

To find the answer, look at Jesus Christ. Look long
with the eyes both of your mind and of your heart.

He was born in the most rigidly ethnic culture of
all time; born in a fiercely nationalistic nation; reared
in Galilee, the most bigoted backwoods area of that nation; born into a family of snobbish royal lineage; born
in a time when revolutionary fanaticism fired every
heart with hatred for the Roman oppressors; born in a
country practicing the apartheid of rigid segregation
between Jews and Samaritans.

Yet He showed not a trace of bigotry.

I challenge you to read and reread the documents
of His life. There is nothing, absolutely nothing, that

1. Gordon Allport, *The Nature of Prejudice* (Garden City: Double-
day, 1954), p. 143.

you can find to indicate any feelings of racial superiority, national prejudice, or personal discrimination.

He taught, "Love your neighbor as yourself." He lived it. "Greater love hath no man than this," He once said, "that a man lay down his life for his friends" (John 15:13, KJV). He did it. He summed up His goals in life with these words: "The Spirit of the Lord is on me, because he has anointed me to preach good news to the poor. He has sent me to proclaim freedom for the prisoners and recovery of sight to the blind, to release the oppressed, to announce the year when the Lord's favor." (Luke 4:18-19, NIV).

He died for it. He died as the victim of prejudiced hatreds, sentenced at a trial without defense, condemned by those who had prejudged Him by their own prejudices, executed by the prejudices of His peers.

Those who stand on the side of Jesus Christ reject prejudice whenever, however, and wherever they find it. In themselves first of all; then, and only then, in the world about them.

What will this mean? Making friends—across racial lines. Why should you have only white (or black, or brown, or yellow) friends? Why advance the cause of prejudice by limiting your friendships to "your kind"?

It will mean going where the barriers are. Refuse to go to a one-race-only church. Avoid restaurants and businesses that serve only one kind of people. Welcome families of other races to move into your block. If you employ, hire on the basis of actual qualifications only, not on phony fears of color problems.

If you say you love your neighbor, live it—as Jesus did—without prejudging your neighbor by your prejudices.

That is the first step toward the open acceptance of others that is so basic to the forgiving style of life.

The second step—stop judging by your biases. This is an even more subtle temptation. It's the habit we often consider an asset, when it may be our greatest liability. It's the automatic reflex of judging others that takes place as we label—and libel—all those around us.

The second beam in the eye is a judgmental mindset.

Were you ever heard to say, "Look, it's obvious that the guy's subversive; he's a Communist"? Or was it, "Listen, that fellow's such a conservative—such an extremist—he's got two right hands"?

Or don't you use labels, read labels, or stick them on others? You must feel a bit lonely. All your friends use labels, don't they? In fact, they likely have a label for you, too.

Strange how quickly we learn to label and how habitually we practice it. From the first childhood labels to the more sophisticated adult classifications, all that's changed is the vocabulary. The mentality is the same, and so is the effect.

Words are wonderful things as long as they are symbols for thought. But once you convert your words from symbols to labels, they replace thought.

Labels are not only a sign of mental stagnation in the user, they aren't exactly healthy for the person labeled either.

To begin with, they're seldom true. Labels are libels. In print, there's only a one-letter difference between *label* and *libel*. In speech, there's usually less. It may be just a wrinkled nose or a raised eyebrow. All it takes to paste someone with a label is an ordinary word smeared with just the right inflection of the voice, contortion of the face, or distortion of the truth.

Labels are libels because they are irrational—illogical. Any textbook of elementary logic begins by demanding that you discard your labels and pastepot because "labels are the most common and foolish logical fallacy." And they are. A label is a weasel word. It's as two-faced or many-faced as users and hearers.

Labels are libels because nine times out of ten they're dishonest. Politicians use them to smear opponents, debaters employ them to brace up weak arguments, and shallow thinkers use them to pretend intelligence.

Well, that's all true, but that's how others use labels, that's not you or I! You and I use labels because they're handy things for sorting out people. A people-watcher has got to have various classifications, and names and labels too, if he or she is going to make some sense out of the human race, right?

And yet, that's exactly where labels shortchange us most. When we use them as cubbyholes—categories—nice little shelves where we stick people for good. "I've got his number," we say. "He's one of that kind." But you can't simplify people like that!

Although, let's admit, we spend a lot of time trying. How often have you heard it said, "There are just two kinds of people in this world—" Well, that's right. There are only two kinds: those who think there are two kinds, and those who think there are more.

Someone remarked rather cynically once, "There are only two kinds of people on earth: the good and the bad. And the good decide which are which."

That's getting at the root of the problem. Most folks believe that they are good enough to criticize and categorize others into their proper classes. So they go on and on, pigeonholing each other under appropriate labels and closing the door to understanding, acceptance, friendship, and brotherly love.

As one sage put it, "Great minds discuss ideals; average minds discuss events; small minds discuss people."

Criticizing another rarely gives us a valid insight into life and living. Certainly criticism inspires feelings, but they're feelings of superiority, not sympathy. No, in most critical comments about people, there's more enmity than empathy. Like the husband asking his wife, "Say, have you heard the latest about Myrtle?" "Heard it?" she replies, "I started it."

We criticize because it does something for us. Something we're not willing to name and face, but something that makes us feel good—for the moment.

This should reveal to us that chronic, critical attitudes are actually symptoms of emotional disturbance. The knocker, complainer, belittler, or gossiper is sick. People who make trouble are generally troubled people. People pick at others to salve their own feelings of guilt by pointing out others who are worse than they; or to scapegoat others for faults they find difficult to own up to in themselves; or to ease emotional tensions and frustrations within their own personalities; or to fulfill their own wishes and desires in imagination, since they cannot or will not do them in act.

Are you brave enough to check this out in yourself? May I give you a little test?

True or false: Do you ever criticize in order to justify your own failure or frustration? You didn't get what you want, or you lost what you had. And so you turned on innocent people who stood in the way? Or passed the buck for your misfortune to some third party?

True or false: Do you ever criticize in order to climb toward your ambition? Do you ever wish misfortune on enemies, competitors, or persons who threaten your success? Do you let your gossip trample on those who get in your way? Do you belittle those beneath you to win approval of those above you?

True or false: Do you ever criticize in order to quiet your guilt feelings or to minimize your own guilt and responsibility? Do you conform to the majority against your better knowledge, and then gossip and criticize the minority whose honest stand made you feel guilty? Do you habitually pick on those who get caught for doing what you got away with?

You can grade yourself on this test, just so you know the score. But didn't it verify your suspicion that your interest in nit-picking others has emotional roots? That chronic criticism is only a symptom of much deeper problems? That at the root it's a moral matter?

It allows us to fulfill our worst inclinations by proxy. Example: William Causins, professor at the Seattle Institute of Real Estate Management, recommends that landlords "keep at least one scandalous couple in each apartment building to keep tenants happy. The presence of such a pair," he insists, "gives tenants something to gossip about and subconsciously makes them happy."

And criticism can be a moral problem for both the talker and the listener. It takes two to backbite. The listener is just as guilty as the speaker. Who can stand by while an absent, and likely innocent, person is dirtied? It is a human responsibility to protest the smearing of a fellow human. Why not gently say, "I'd rather not listen to the criticism of another when she's not present to defend herself." Or ask, "Why do you think I should be told this story about him?"

If you know something that would hurt or hinder the life or reputation of another, bury it. Forget it. End it right there. It will rest in peace. So will you.

If you "love your neighbor," remember, "love covers over a multitude of sins" (1 Peter 4:8, NIV). Love can even remove a beam of malice from a critical eye.

Love heals. Love encourages. Love protects. Love looks for the best in others so that others may be their best.

The late, great Christian A. W. Tozer has suggested a way through this problem. "Vow: Never to pass on anything about anybody else that will hurt him in any way."[2]

Jesus said:

> Don't criticize people, and you will not be criticized. For you will be judged by the way you criticize others, and the measure you give will be the measure you receive. Why do you look at the speck of sawdust in your brother's eye and fail to notice the plank in your own? How can you say to your brother, "Let me get the speck out of your eye," when there is a plank in your own? You fraud! Take the plank out of your own eye first, and then you can see clearly enough to remove your brother's speck of dust. (Matthew 7:1-5)

Summarizing these words of Christ, William Barclay suggests three great reasons why no one can judge another.

1. We never know the whole facts or the whole person. We cannot understand the circumstances or temptations.
2. It is almost impossible for any one to be strictly impartial in judgment.
3. No one is good enough to judge any other. Our own faults and our own inability to resolve them automatically disqualify us as fair critics.[3]

2. A. W. Tozer, *Five Vows for Spiritual Power* (Harrisburg, Pa.: Christian Publishing, n.d.), p. 12.
3. William Barclay, *The Daily Study Bible* (Edinburgh: St. Andrew, 1962), pp. 266-68.

Well, that is all true, but there are times when we must judge. What then?

We must judge and criticize lovingly—for the purpose of helping, lifting, and redeeming, not to punish or get even. We must judge honestly, admitting where we too are guilty of the same fault and dealing as severely with ourselves as with others. We must criticize humbly, realizing that our own lives are open to the scrutiny of the Judge of all the earth.

Only when we attempt to judge in honesty, in humility, and in charity are our own eyes clear. Only then is the plank of an unloving, malicious, or vengeful spirit removed. Only then is the beam of our own sinful actions and attitudes withdrawn. Then we can see our way clear to remove the splinter in the other's eye. Not to label it and give a sister or brother a sore eye, but to offer the hand of help—and healing.

That's accepting others as persons, treating them as fellow human beings in need of the mercy and love of God and demonstrating forgiveness even in criticism. Don't we owe them the loving, understanding, forgiving help of one all-too-human human being to another? After all, that's the kind of merciful, compassionate love God showed us in Jesus Christ. And Jesus Christ gives that same strength to love and forgive to all those who open their lives to Him, those who risk taking the label *Christian* to follow Him daily in life.

9

FORGIVENESS IN ACTION

We all caught our breath as the waitress fumbled the plates of dessert, then dropped one across the shoulder of the guest of honor. The cake and lemon sauce spread a wide smear down his coat, tie, and shirt and ended in his lap.

In a few moments, this man, an outstanding Christian and a United States senator, was to stand and speak to the five hundred guests of this prayer breakfast. Now he was trying with a dinner knife to lift off the gooey mess. The waitress returned with towels, and tried in her embarrassment to undo the slip of a hand.

The look on her face was pure pain. She wanted to die! The senator's murmuring, "It's OK. It'll be all right," didn't seem to help.

When the last bit of lemon sauce was wiped away, and the girl gathered her towels to go, the senator reached out both hands to touch her still red face, drew her down, and gently kissed her cheek. The blush disappeared. A smile took its place. She left the room, radiant, head erect, alive.

Then I realized what he had done. He had taken a memory that would hurt painfully for the rest of her life, a memory that would arouse all the feelings of shame and guilt whenever it came back to her, and he had turned that memory into a story she'd love to tell. "Senator Harold Hughes kissed me right there just after I'd dropped a dessert—" she'd be able to say with pride.

What a thousand words of "I forgive you" could not do (they would likely have hurt even more), one gentle act of acceptance did perfectly.

And for me, sitting close enough to see, this little act of forgiving had a greater impact than the one-thousand-word address that followed. His message told the story of a transformed life—his own. It was an excellent witness to the work of God in bringing this man from his own tragedy of alcoholism to a life of healing and rich service.

But the simple kiss of forgiveness was even more powerful. He understood how words may only add to the shame and pain, but a gentle act of acceptance and forgiveness can mean so much more. In forgiving, it is what the person is and does that speaks more than what he or she says.

When the hurt is mutual, as is more often the case, neither person has the right to say a thousand words of "I forgive you," for both need the forgiveness. Then a simple act of love may say it so much better. Like a handclasp that says, "I want to be close again," or a gesture of need that says, "You are important to me; I want your love and respect."

Rarely is the offense or injury one-sided. More often we are both involved to some extent. And we both need forgiveness.

And there's the rub. To say, "I forgive you," can be strangely tainted with superiority. It can conceal a hidden accusation, a judgment. In fact, it usually does. Forgiveness is a decision about an act of wrongdoing. It is a choice of what to do about an offense. To say, "I forgive you," is to say, "I have been wronged, I recognize this as a fact, I am willing to accept the wrongdoing without revenge or resentment." That contains an accusation, a judgment, and a decision on the effects.

And if we are both involved in the offense, both responsible for the hurt, then to say, "I forgive you," is more than a bit self-righteous. Far better, perhaps, to say, "I want to be close again, to accept and be accepted," or, "to forgive and be forgiven."

Forgiveness, most often, needs to be two-way. Mutual. Reciprocal.

Notice all the ways this is said in the Bible:

"Forgive as you have been forgiven."

"Forgive as freely as forgiveness has been given you."

"Ask for forgiveness only in the measure you are willing to extend to others."

"If you do not forgive another his trespasses, neither will you be forgiven."

"Confront another in the awareness of your own weakness, in memory of your own like tendencies to fail or fall."

"Love the other as you love yourself."

"Respect your neighbor as you want to be respected."

Forgiveness is such a two-way street that gentle, but genuine, acceptance is the one truly important first step when there is pain between you and me.

In fact, one great Christian thinker of our time suggested we drop the word *forgiveness* from our vocabulary, since it is so paternalistic, such a superior-to-inferior relationship. "Use the word *acceptance*," he counseled. "It is two-way, it is mutual, it has an honest humility about it."

And that is the point of Jesus' teaching on love for others. Accept them into forgiven right relationships, knowing that you too need acceptance and forgiveness if you are to be in right relationships with God and humanity. (Read Matthew 18:21-35.) And such acceptance is better done with one act of love than with a thousand words.

THE POWER OF FORGIVENESS

To explore how action, not diction, is the most powerful language of forgiveness, let's explore several cases from life. First, a personal profile.

He was born into a talented, highly competitive family: a brilliant father, creative mother, winning sisters, and strong, successful brothers. But he? He looked ordinary, performed average, achieved the usual, won no attention or recognition.

In another family he might have accepted his place as an average, normal, ordinary-contributing Mr. Everybody. But here it was impossible. There were his father's high expectations to deal with, not to mention brother-sister pressures.

College? "Yes," said dad. "No," said son.

He tried a job, business entanglements, financial responsibilities, serious courtship—all as ways of escape.

"No, no, no," said dad.

Finally he played the angry trump card. Quick marriage by elopement. He settled down to his chosen life. Forgot his family. But he found no satisfaction. Now that he had what he had wanted, he discovered it wasn't what he wanted after all. And all the old drives to achieve, to win recognition, awoke within him.

Business success? Blind alley. Social prominence? No admission. That left him one outlet—his church. He poured himself into it. He was missing education, so he used piety.

Piety turned out to be the master stroke. Pious activity could win respect and acclaim. Pious concerns shared as prayer requests could eliminate competitors. Conspicuous good works performed with obvious humility could collect recognition.

Then, just as he was achieving it all, it began to slip through his fingers. So he drove in stakes defensively. He formed stronger convictions, increasing his conservatism and dogmatism. Soon he found himself in the middle of threatening rifts and a schism between him and those valiant for the truth.

Next came charges, accusations, and bitterness.

Did no one understand his battle?

Yes, yes they did. Too well, but all hesitated to approach him. Who could help him see his own conflicts projected on others? Who cared enough to reach out with the attention, the affection, the acceptance early enough while it could still be heard?

There was such a person. A man of deep feeling and intuition who wasn't good with words but great with friendships, fishing rods, and love. Slowly he found himself convicted that this man, who seemed so sure of his rightness, so superior in his goodness, was really fragile, afraid, and hurting behind all the armor.

He took him fishing. He didn't catch any fish, but he listened for a whole day. The man hadn't had anyone hear him out for years, and he loved a good listener. By evening he was at a different place. He had discovered that he needed to go and talk to the person he had been criticizing and accusing most. Our angler had played no angles, he had only been present and at times honestly reflective. He gave him unconditional acceptance, and it came as cool water to a man with deep thirst. He had been starved for attention, and, surprisingly, one day's worth gave him enough nourishment to begin conversation with those he had feared.

What a thousand words could never do in storming defenses, one action did by slipping past the guards. And the man in the fortress came out with his armor down for a short walk, and they truly met.

Case two: He was born into a family of no wealth, no reputation, no respected position in their community—nobodies.

His brothers and sisters—underachievers. Dropouts at grade eight or nine. His father worked only several months out of the year. His mother struggled to keep body and soul together by dishing out what little they had, stitching up what threads they almost no longer had, and, in general, working enough for two people.

Was it anger over his parents' negligent carelessness, their voluntary poverty? Was it humiliation from his peer group's patronizing smiles? Was it sheer frustration from his own deprived way of life? Whatever— or whichever—the reason, he was fired with a new strain of family traits.

He slugged his way through high school, making the highest grades but not becoming valedictorian (not well-rounded enough—besides, you know his family). Somehow he held two jobs—one after school, one weekends. Then came his break into a small business of his own.

He had difficulties socially—seldom with the girl, almost always with the parents. Still he persevered.

Then came marriage. Financial success. Business prominence. Community recognition by people who saw him as the man he had become. But among his old friends and in his church? There he was still the boy from that family, who grew up in that house, on that street.

So he began to press at a few points that were open to challenge in his church. Others who shared his feelings of dissatisfaction gathered around him. The congregation began to divide. Tensions grew. Rumors began to flow, quietly at first. Then accusations broke into the open. Old sneers at his family surfaced and circulated again.

Did no one understand? Truth was not on trial; love was. It was not a conservative-liberal conflict or even the new versus the old. It was the "in's" against the "out's." The establishment versus the intruder.

Did no one come to give the honest acceptance, recognition, and love needed or deserved? Was no one willing to see him for what he wanted to be, for what he had worked to become, for what he now was?

Did no one care?

There was someone. This time it was a pastor who recognized that this man not only had gifts, he had a deep urgency to contribute to the life of the church and to its ministry in the community.

He could have spent two years in weekly sessions of pastoral psychotherapy with this man to help him sort out the roots of his anger, the dynamics of his conflicts with others, the mixed motives in his concerns about the church. It would all have been accurate, insightful, perhaps reconciling. It might have ended in forgiveness and healing. But he chose another way.

He invited the man to enter a two-year teacher-disciple contract and became a supportive mentor. He delegated ministry tasks suited to his gifts, outlined training experiences, went to seminars with him, and watched him grow. Halfway into the second year, the man sold his business and went to seminary. There conviction was sharpened into clarity of faith, urgency was tempered into resources of love and compassion to aid others in their growth. His life was transformed over a five-year period, and the ministry he now offers to others is a gift of God.

It is not what the pastor said, although there were many words of wisdom in what he offered. It was who he was and what he did. He gave attention. He was available. He embodied the acceptance and forgiveness the man needed. He gave him a second chance at life. The man had painted himself into a corner with no exits. The pastor swung him a rope.

Case three: She was Ms. Average Citizen. Average home. Average education. Average wealth. Normal. Usual. Run-of-the-mill. Not that she was Ms. Nobody. She was Ms. Everybody.

But now and again she grew dissatisfied. Not that she consciously decided in those times, "I'm gonna throw my weight around a little." No, it was just that she had to lean the weight of her frustrations somewhere.

So she'd find herself agitating a little, criticizing a bit, or "sharing a concern," as it is sometimes called.

She could apply a little pressure to get something changed just to make her presence felt. She could point out some problem or oversight, find some fault to rub with salt—to show that even she knew better than that and to let those on top hear from the rest of humanity.

She could quote a few appropriate criticisms when frustrations needed to be brought out into the open. She could anonymously stir the troubled waters that lie beneath the surface of any group. Not maliciously, mind you, but out of the frustration of being a taken-for-granted bit of the social backwaters.

And in her church, where the social machine often ran without much lubrication of love, her refusing to be a smoothly meshing cog in the machine generated friction—with both heat and wear. In this case, her frustrations went unnoticed, her needs unmet, and the church suffered.

Of all places, a church should have an abundance of persons who recognize needs in each other and seek to meet them. People who can pick up the pieces, piece them together again into wholeness, oneness, rightness, and unity—that's what the work of forgiving and reconciling is.

THE POWER OF PEACEMAKING

"Happy are the peacemakers," Jesus once said, "because they are called God's sons."

Yes. They are. They are people who recognize the God of peace as their father, the Prince of Peace as their leader, and the way of peacemaking as the only Christlike way of life and look for actions to take that include others, deeds to perform that assert the value of others.

They run the risk of stepping into moments of conflict to do curative peace work, to heal torn relationships, and even do a bit of surgery where needed.

And they're also concerned about preventive peacemaking. They look for building hostilities and help to relieve them while they're still forming, before they reach the explosive stage.

They take action in such simple yet powerful ways.

First, they judge others, not by what they've been or what they've done, but by what they are now.

> The very spring of our actions is the love of Christ
> ... This means that our knowledge of men can no
> longer be based on their outward lives (indeed, even
> though we knew Christ as a man we do not know
> him like that any longer). For if a man is in Christ he

becomes a new person altogether—the past is finished and gone, everything has become fresh and new. (2 Corinthians 5:14a, 16-17)

Second, they look for strengths in others and encourage them. They sense where there are gifts and talents lying dormant or ignored and try to release them. As the Bible says:

For just as you have many members in one physical body and those members differ in their functions, so we, though many in number, compose one body in Christ and are all members of one another. . . .
    Let us have no imitation Christian love. Let us have a genuine break with evil and a real devotion to good. Let us have real warm affection for one another as between brothers, and a willingness to let the other man have the credit. (Romans 12:4-5, 10)

To look for opportunities of building, of encouraging, of helping release others to become all they can be in Christ is worth a thousand words of advice.

To share concern for the other's fulfillment, self-discovery, opportunity for service, and meaningful work is better than a thousand criticisms or compliments.

Like our Master, we who follow Jesus are people who act in love, knowing love is something you do as well as think and feel. So they look for actions of reconciling, forgiving, and healing. As did Christ.

Notice. When someone loses control of his anger and slaps your face in rage, Jesus calls you to act out your forgiveness. Jesus was saying, "Stay vulnerable." Turn an unprotected cheek to say, "I'm not going to back away from you, because our relationship matters too much to build walls of defense between us. A second cheek, going a second mile, giving up a second coat, offering a second chance—all these are acts of acceptance. Acts that move us one step toward reconciliation.

Jesus was a master at simple acts that spoke a million words.

To establish a relationship with an outcast minority-group woman, a questionable person in her own society, Jesus simply placed Himself in the position of needing and asking for a favor—"May I have a drink of water from the pitcher you have just drawn from the deep well?" But in that act, He set aside social custom, racial prejudice, religious traditions, class distinctions, male-female barriers, and superior-inferior attitudes and fears.

It was a simple act of acceptance, of bridging the two-way need for forgiveness between two nations locked in fear and avoidance of each other.

Such unexpected acts of acceptance were His way of life. He invited Himself to dinner with the despised tax collector. He gave caring acceptance in clear acts of love.

Understand, He was no "nice guy" trying to earn everybody's approval and make everybody love Him. He could be surgically sharp when surgery was the loving thing to do. His acts, like going to the cross, have touched off millions of spoken and written words, trying to express the depth of such caring for others. But the acts remain clearer than all the words.

And so it is in our relationships. To forgive, to accept, to move again into right relationships, to be brothers and sisters again, is not a matter of words. It is deeds, acts, gestures of love.

It is simple steps of acceptance—caring enough to feel the other's pain for a moment and then doing for the other what you would want done for you. It is respecting the other's needs as you respect your own. It is meeting the other on the common ground you share, not demanding that he or she come over on my turf, see things from my point of view, and live or forgive as I prescribe. It is recognizing the other's needs to live accepted and forgiven, as you too need to be accepted and forgiven.

It requires mutual acts of love given through loving behavior.

Although I've just written a thousand words about loving, accepting, and forgiving acts, one act would say it better.

Forgiveness in action is love enacted—embodied seventy times seven.

10

FORGIVENESS AND THE ENEMY

May Haviland, a member of the Society of Friends
—a Quaker—showed the power of love to surprise and
overpower evil. She opened the door of her room one
night and was astounded to see a burly, dark-haired
man rifling her bureau drawers. Quietly she entered
the room and closed the door behind her. At the faint
click the burglar wheeled, pistol in hand.

"Put that thing down," she said, "I'm going to help
you because you must need whatever I have much
more than I do, if you have to steal for it."

The burglar, dumbfounded, watched as she opened
a secret drawer and pressed her jewelry on him, telling
him she was sorry that his need was so urgent. Suddenly the man dropped his gun and fled, taking nothing.

The next day, an unsigned note was in her mail-
box. It read: "Madam, I have known only hate and
fear. I can deal with them. But I was powerless before
your kindness."

Retelling it, May added, "Even guns are silent in
the face of love."

Forgiving love has a strange power, the power to include the enemy, to refuse to let the enemy define who is what and what is what. Another may define himself or herself as the enemy, but love refuses the definition.

Love retains the power to confront alienation not with further alienation but with acceptance and compassion.

These are strange words in Western culture. We have come to trust violence as the last word in resolving our difficulties.

"Americans not only condone violence, we love it. We love to fight," says Dr. David Abrahamsen, a researcher in violence at Brandeis University. "Violence by gun is an American trait. We are still living under the legend of the Wild West where action with a gun— was the easiest solution."[1]

Stanford University psychologist Albert Bandura pinpoints why. "The whole culture has changed the violence syndrome into a cool guiltless routine of disposing of problems by disposing of the people who cause the problem."[2]

In a recent year in America some six thousand persons died of gunshot wounds. Contrast this with Great Britain, where there were fewer than thirty; France, under twenty; Belgium, less than a dozen.

"We are a violent people with a violent history," says Arthur Schlesinger, Jr., the Pulitzer prize winning historian and aide to the assassinated President Kennedy. "The instinct for violence has seeped into the blood stream of our national life."[3]

1. David Abrahamsen, "Hostility," *Daily News Record* (Harrisonburg, Va.), 12 June 1968.
2. Ibid.
3. Ibid.

Violence is among us on many levels. There is the hidden violence of injustice that forces people to be less than human. The violence of prejudice that dashes a group's hopes for happiness, shatters self-respect, and thwarts life's meaning. That's not violent, you say? Just ask the blacks. They can tell you.

This sort of hidden viciousness then breaks into open violence against persons or property. People all around us are advocating it. As one spokesman told a rally in Raleigh, North Carolina, "We don't believe in violence, and we don't intend to have any violence if we have to kill every Negro in America." That's what the man said.

Or, in response, there is the violence advocated by the impatient or disillusioned liberal who, as Robert Fitch puts it, "tremulously anticipates violence before it occurs, celebrates it while it is happening, and justifies it when it is over."[4]

WHY THE VIOLENCE AMONG US?

Some say the violence in our culture springs from impatience. The impatience of those whose dreams and ideals turn to despair. Others say affluence, prosperity, and permissiveness have made pleasure-seekers and power-seekers out of us all. Still others say its cause is frustration. "Our society is built on success. Success, measured by materialism, creates frustration. Frustration is the wet nurse of violence."

Those who probe deeper say violence is simply hatred acted out. John Gardner, former Secretary of Health, Education, and Welfare, writes, "Hatred triggers violence, violence stirs further hatred, savage re-

4. Robert Fitch, "Is America Really Sick?" *U.S. News and World Report* (10 June 1968): 47.

sponses, hostility begets hostility, and the storm rages on. At some point, the terrifying interplay must have an end."[5]

If anything comes natural, it's the urge to get even. To deliver insult for insult, blow for blow, injury for injury. The law of tit for tat is the oldest law in the world. It is found in the earliest recorded law code, the code of Hammurabi, from ancient Babylon (almost four thousand years old). It is cited in almost all systems of law, including the Jewish (Exodus 21:23-25; Leviticus 24:19-20; Deuteronomy 19:21).

And it seems like simple fair play. An eye must be paid with an eye. It's second nature to demand it of the enemy.

But Jesus said, "You've always heard it said: an eye for an eye, and a tooth for a tooth; but I tell you, don't resist evil; but if anyone strikes you on the right cheek, turn the other to him also" (Matthew 5:38-39, paraphrase).

"We Communists have many things in common with the teachings of Jesus Christ," Nikita Khrushchev, ex-premier of Russian, once stated to American pressmen. He continued, "My sole difference with Christ is that when someone hits me on the right cheek, I hit him on the left so hard that his head falls off."[6]

Perhaps more people have tripped over Christ's statement about turning the other cheek and turned away from faith than over any other demand He made.

No retaliation? No revenge? No repayment? To the angry it's a ridiculous demand. It denies us our

5. John Gardner, "Hostility," *Daily News Record* (Harrisonburg, Va.), 12 June 1968.
6. Nikita Khrushchev, as cited by Stewart Meachem in address given to Intercollegiate Peace Fellowship, Bluffton College, Bluffton, Ohio, March 31, 1960.

most basic right—the right of self-defense. "Self-defense has become not only a right, but a duty," an American writer wrote recently. That's a proper opinion to most men who speak of "the manly art of self-defense" as if it were an unalienable right of humanity or to women who trust the protection of a "Saturday night special" as essential.

When violence is seen as the necessary safeguard for personal security, we all lose. To equate violence with personal strength is an illusion. It requires far greater strength to practice nonviolence than to let anger follow the natural course to explosive retaliation or coercion.

In personal conflicts, it's usually the one in the wrong who clenches a fist first. It's the one who is beaten mentally and morally who tries to settle it with muscle or maneuvering. When a person is wrong and knows it, temper is bound to flare, fists clench, knuckles whiten. Violence is usually an unconscious confession of weakness, inferiority, and cowardice in facing up to the true state of things. In the long view, violence is, has been, and always will be the loser's way.

Violence and *victory* are contradictory. When one strikes another down, the winner wins nothing but defeat.

Violence never resolves violence. Hate cannot overcome hate. Evil is never destroyed by evil. It may be temporarily arrested or postponed, but payday comes. Revenge is always self-defeating. The only antidote to hate is love. Only goodness can extinguish the fires of evil.

If you let the other person's evil actions determine your reactions, or let another's violence move you to violence, you lose the opportunity of helping and healing that comes only through love.

So what do you do when you feel the sting on your cheek?

"Oh, but I've got my rights," you may say. And you're right. If you strike back, you can claim, "I was justified in what I did. I did nothing that he did not do to me first."

And that may well be true. If you intend to claim all your rights in life, to even all scores against you, to demand every penny ever owed you, then go ahead.

But if you give no inch, expect no second chances; if you show no mercy, do not hope for mercy; if you extend no forgiveness, you can expect none. Life, love, mercy, and forgiveness are all two-way streets. To receive you must give humbly, aware of the fact that you are constantly in need of the understanding and acceptance of others and the loving mercy of God.

FINDING THE WAY OF JESUS

"All they that take the sword shall perish by the sword," said Jesus Christ. Is there any doubt?

In contrast to our human way of violence, Christ called us to unclench fists and learn the power of love. "But I tell you, Do not resist an evil person. . . . Love your enemies and pray for those who persecute you, that you may be sons of your Father in heaven" (Matthew 5:39, 44-45, NIV).

His disciples apparently took Him at His word. For the first two hundred years of Christianity not only nonviolence but nonresistance was the practice of Christians. The church not only survived; it grew in great numbers and strength through three centuries of nonresistance to vicious persecution.

The Christian who seeks to follow Christ in life today chooses the way of nonviolent, nonresistant love as did the Master. The Master refused violence, and so must we.

We refuse violence because we also know that love alone can conquer hatred. Only love can defeat violence. *Love* is the last word.

The person who follows Christ chooses the way of nonviolence because God is on the side of justice. God and justice will triumph in the end. No evil means can assist. That was Christ's conviction.

The Bible says, "When he suffered, he made no threats. Instead, he entrusted himself to him who judges justly" (1 Peter 2:23, NIV).

This total faith in God's eternal future lets those who make Christ's way their own accept suffering without violence and revenge. This was the way of Christ. Is it not to be our way, too?

We who love retaliation and revenge can be thankful that God does not! When God walked among us in Jesus Christ, He lived—and called us to live—in a far different way. He chose to show patience, even at the cost of suffering. He chose to forgive, even at the cost of His life. All this because of love.

So the person who follows Christ in living by love responds differently to the person who abuses. Sure he cares when someone slaps his face, but he cares more about the other person than about the insult. By turning the other cheek he is saying, "What I care about is *you*, friend. I don't want you to go on in bitter, harsh anger. I may have the human right to strike back, but I pass it by because I feel a responsibility for you before God. I take the humiliating, defenseless way but not out of cowardice. Obviously it demands more bravery and more strength of character to control anger than to obey it. But I refuse to retaliate because *you* are far more important. Your discovery of the love and forgiveness of God is of greater value than my getting even."

Obviously, that's no easy thing to do or say. In small insults that matter little, it's possible and practical. But in the harsh, painful conflicts when you feel the full weight of the other's contempt, it's almost impossible.

And Christ *was* speaking of the lowest expression of contempt. "If a man strikes you on the *right* cheek," He says. What does that mean? If you are right-handed, you would naturally strike another on the left cheek. To strike on the right would demand an awkward contortion—unless you struck disdainfully with the back of the hand. In Christ's time, as in ours, to slap another with the back of your hand was a doubly insulting, arrogant flick of hate.

"To even the lowest of insults," said Christ, "turn the other cheek; accept the insult without resentment."

Did Christ practice this Himself? When slapped inhumanely, He accepted it unhesitatingly, unflinchingly, turning the other cheek even as He asked, "If I said something wrong, testify as to what is wrong. But if I spoke the truth, why did you strike me?" (John 18:23, NIV). He gladly gave up the right to defend Himself in order to speak in defense of the truth.

Peter, who stood by watching, later wrote: "When he was insulted he offered no insult in return. When he suffered he made no threats of revenge. He simply committed his cause to the one who judges fairly" (1 Peter 2:23).

To this Paul added: "Never take vengeance into your own hands, my dear friends: stand back and let God punish if he will: For it is written: Vengeance belongeth unto me: I will recompense" (Romans 12:19).

And these are God's words: "If thine enemy hunger, feed him; If he thirst, give him to drink: For in so doing thou shalt heap coals of fire upon his head. Don't allow yourself to be overpowered with evil. Take the offensive—overpower evil with good!" (Romans 12:20-21).

That is the strategy of the utterly unexpected. Such love has a scalding, humbling power.

For example, a Canadian friend once wrote me: "I once slapped a Christian's face during a conversation we had. He got me mad. I had anger in me, and I slapped him. When I did, he turned the other cheek. I had no courage to slap again. I was stunned."

"But," you ask, "if I turn the other cheek, how do I know it will work?" There is no guarantee of effectiveness. It may not result in moving you toward reconciliation.

After all, love is not a strategy. It is a way of life. The life of love modeled by Jesus. We do not follow it because it is more secure, but because it is moral, it is principled, it is faithful to the values we believe are eternal.

Obviously, it's a difficult way. Any appeal to the enemy's conscience bears great risk. But so do all the valuable things in life. The choice to love is the most risky choice in the universe. But in the end, it is the only alternative that will endure. Of all our motivations and decisions, only love endures.

In a world of violence the most viable alternative, the most valid approach, is the way of Christ. It's the way of love—peacemaking, nonviolent, nonresistant love.

Only a Christianity of love can survive with integrity in an age of violence. It alone can be Christian if being faithful to the way of Jesus is the mark of authentic Christianity.

Thus, we may conclude, all Christians are peacemakers; indeed, pacifists, since all believe that the cross,

not the sword, is God's last word; that love and forgiveness, not coercion and violence, are the heart of the
gospel. The difference among Christians is not over
this central issue, but over how much provocation is
necessary, how much justification is required before
one lays down the way of Jesus and resorts to the way
of violence. There are followers of Jesus who are willing to suffer very little threat before they become prag-
matic and justify the use of violence to insure safety on
their own terms. In contrast, some followers believe
that the way of Jesus can be embraced without resort-
ing to the use of force at any point.

Jesus' words are unmistakable, the voice of the
New Testament is clear, the practice of the early church
is consistent—nonviolent love is the Jesus way. We must
choose. Will we risk following the way of Christ in enemy love? Or join our culture in justifying violent alter-
natives?

Will forgiveness be our first and last word, as it
was for our Lord? Or will it be used when it seems ad-
visable, defensible, practical?

Or do we forgive, seventy times seven?

11

FORGIVENESS AND MUTUAL LOVE

I arrived in the city of Everywhere early one morning. It was cold, and there were flurries of snow on the ground. As I stepped from the train to the platform I noticed that the baggageman and the redcap were warmly attired in heavy coats and gloves, but oddly enough, they wore no shoes. Repressing my impulse to ask the reason for this odd practice, I went into the station and inquired the way to the hotel. My curiosity, however, was increased by the discovery that no one in the station wore any shoes. Boarding the streetcar, I saw that my fellow travelers were likewise barefoot; and upon arriving at the hotel I found that the bellhop, the clerk, and the residents were all devoid of shoes.

Unable to restrain myself longer, I asked the manager what the practice meant.

"What practice?" said he.

"Why," said I, pointing to his bare feet, "why don't you wear shoes in this town?"

"Ah," said he, "that is just it. Why don't we?"

"But what is the matter? Don't you believe in shoes?"

"Believe in shoes, my friend! I should say we do. That is the first article of our creed, shoes. They are indispensable to the well-being of humanity. Such frostbite, cuts, sores, and suffering as shoes prevent! It is wonderful!"

"Well, then, why don't you wear them?" I asked, bewildered.

"Ah," he said thoughtfully, "that is just it. Why don't we?"

Though considerably nonplussed I checked in, secured my room, and went directly to the coffee shop. There I deliberately sat down by an amiable-looking but barefoot gentleman. Friendly enough, he suggested, after we had eaten, that we look about the city.

The first thing we noticed upon emerging from the hotel was a huge brick structure of impressive proportions. He pointed to this with pride.

"You see that?" said he. "That is one of our outstanding shoe manufacturing establishments!"

"A *what?*" I asked in amazement. "You mean you make shoes there?"

"Well, not exactly," said he, a bit abashed. "We talk about making shoes there, and, believe me, we have one of the most brilliant young fellows you have ever heard. He talks most thrillingly and convincingly every week on this great subject of shoes. Just yesterday he moved the people profoundly with his exposition of the necessity of shoe wearing. Many broke down and wept. It was really wonderful!"

"But why don't they wear them?" said I insistently.

"Ah, that is just it. Why don't we?"

Just then, as we turned down a side street, I saw through a cellar window a cobbler actually making a pair of shoes. Excusing myself from my friend, I burst into the little shop and asked the shoemaker how it happened that his shop was not over-run with customers. "Nobody wants my shoes," he said. "They just talk about them."

"Give me what pairs you have ready," I said eagerly, and paid him thrice the amount he modestly asked. Hurriedly I returned to my friend and offered them to him, saying, "Here, my friend, one of these pairs will surely fit you. Take them, put them on. They will save untold suffering."

"Ah, thank you," he said, with embarrassment, "but you don't understand. It just isn't being done. The front families, well, that is just it. Why don't we?"

And coming out of the city of Everywhere, over and over and over that question rang in my ears: "Why don't we? Why don't we? Why don't we?"

*   *   *

The parable of the barefoot Christians was written more than a hundred years ago by an English clergyman, Hugh Price Hughes. The city he calls Everywhere could be Boston, Houston, Toronto, or Toledo—as well as London or Dublin. It is anywhere. It is everywhere. It is where people know of the most basic, obvious steps toward right relationships but do not take them. The shoes on their feet are to be the good news of peace (Ephesians 6:15), yet they go barefoot.

The most basic footwear of life is the rule of mutual love, often called "the law of reciprocity" or "the golden rule."

"Act toward your neighbor as you would want your neighbor to act toward you."

The goal of adult maturation is to achieve mutuality, that state in which other's needs become considered alongside one's own. The goal of adult love is to arrive at a point, as Harry Stack Sullivan used to say, where another's safety and security are as important as one's own. The goal of Christian spirituality is to come to the place where our neighbor's needs and welfare are as high a concern as our own wants and wishes.

All these are contained in the words we call the golden rule.

It is the best known, most frequently quoted statement of the greatest figure in history—Jesus Christ. When first given nineteen centuries ago, it came as a summarization of the entire Jewish law on "how to live with humans." It is still unsurpassed as a basic rule in human relations and worthy of the wisest thinker's consideration.

Let's think it through together, shall we?

First of all, is it not a universal rule of life?

The idea of a fair basis of concern and respect for others is an old one, a multicultural one that emerges in many religious traditions and in many cultural world views.

Confucius said, "What you do not want done to yourself, do not do to others."

Zoroaster, the ancient Persian, taught that "nature alone is good which refrains from doing unto another whatsoever is not good for itself."

Hinduism: "This is the sum of duty: Do naught unto others which would cause you pain if done to you."

Buddhism: "Hurt not others in ways that you yourself would find hurtful."

Judaism: "What is hateful to yourself, do to no other. That is the entire law; all the rest is commentary."

The Greek philosophers each had his own way of phrasing it. Epictetus: "What thou avoidest suffering thyself seek not to impose on others." Socrates: "Do not do to others what would anger you if done to you by others."

Jesus gave the law of reciprocity a different perspective. Rather than offering it as a prohibition, He gave it as a commission.

"Treat other people exactly as you would like to be treated by them—this is the essence of all true religion" (Matthew 7:12).

The newness, the uniqueness of Christ's positive rule of life lies in the commission to act lovingly, to do the thoughtful, considerate, sympathetic thing.

It is not unique just because it is a positive action. Even beneficial actions can rise from evil motives. Positive actions can be positively wrong.

Consider the way it has been twisted in the proposition that "business is business." The golden rule is changed to "Do unto others before they do it to you."

In warfare the rule is positive yet destructive. "In war," says Dr. MacIver, professor of political science at Columbia University, "the principle must be do to the enemy as he would do to you, but do it first."[1] (That's merely the savage law of retaliation. "Do back to others as they have done to you." Or even worse, "Do to others as you expect them to do to you.")

What a vast difference between the human reaction of doing as we are done by, and Christ's call to do as we would wish to be done by. Christ's standard, do as *you* wish from others, provides an unselfish rule of thumb for deciding your actions and attitudes to others.

The golden rule is balanced to protect both sides against the selfishness that always lurks beneath the surface of human beings. There are moral philosophers who point out that the rule should read, "Do unto oth-

---

1. Ernest Trice Thompson, *Sermon on the Mount* (Richmond: Knox, 1946), pp. 117-18.

ers as they would have you do unto them." They insist that Christ's wording, "Do as you would have them do to you," is self-centered, drawing the lines by what you want instead of what your neighbor wants.

But to always do what your neighbor wants or asks would not be love; it would be neutrality, disinterest, or indifference to the other's good. It would be a servile slavery to another's wishes.

A doctor would give heroin to an addict because he wants it; a girl would surrender sex to a boy because he asks it.

That is not love, as any parent knows. Love is a concern for your neighbor. So if you love, give and do for another as you wish to be treated.

The benchmark for your action—do what *you* wish from others—comes out again and again in Christ's teaching. In fact, the golden rule is simply the practical application of the second greatest of all commandments: "To love your neighbor as yourself."

You are to love yourself. The Bible gives that command over a dozen times. Your self-respect should be so high that not for the world—or for anything in it—will you stoop to demean your character or do a deed unworthy of yourself. Hold yourself in high regard, Christ taught, but no higher than you hold your neighbor.

In the biblical vision, love for self and love for neighbor are not two loves, but one and the same love with two different aspects. The same basis by which I know myself to be precious is equally true for you. To love oneself rightly is to love the other equally.

Christ applied this rule to the most crucial areas of life. In love: love your neighbor as you love yourself (Matthew 22:39). In forgiveness: forgive your brother as you wish to be forgiven (6:14-15). In service: do to others as you would have them do to you (7:12).

THE GOLDEN RULE IN ACTION

You've just settled down for a comfortable evening at home. Then your sister phones you. "Can't you come over and talk with Bill," she says. "He's really got the blues."

"It's pretty bad, eh?" you ask, hedging, remembering all the times she's called for help in the last weeks and you've given her a string of excuses. Well, that's when she breaks all to pieces.

"Please," she says, "he's so down in the dumps he'll hardly talk, and when he does, he scares the life out of me."

"What do you mean?" you ask her. "Is he—?"

"Yes," she says breaking in. "He's talking about quitting everything again. Walking out on his work, giving up on all his payments, and maybe even—on life."

"On life?"

"Uh-huh!"

"You mean he's talking suicide again?"

"Yes, and this time—I can't explain it. I just feel that he means it."

"Now look," you say with a bit of guilty irritation. "You've got to get him to a doctor."

"Heaven knows I've tried," she says. "But he just won't budge." And then she does what you've been expecting. She puts the squeeze on you.

"Please," she says, "won't you come over tonight and try to talk with him? *Please.*"

"Oh, now," you say, "I've told you I'm no good at that. You'll have to count me out."

"Oh, but you've got to come," she insists. "You're the only guy in the family that he really trusts."

"Let me think about it," you say.

But she says, "No. Don't try to put me off. There just isn't time. Something terrible is going to happen."

So there you are—on the phone—and now on the hook. Shall you go talk to that brother-in-law considering suicide? Or back out once and for all?

How do we live the golden rule in daily action?

We listen to others as we want to be listened to. We offer help to others where we would expect help. We seek to understand others' viewpoints as we would be understood. We care more about dealing fairly with our neighbor than we worry about being cheated by our neighbor.

We offer praise and appreciation to others, as we want to be appreciated. We treat employees, creditors, and debtors as we wish to be treated by those over us. We pass on no gossip about another that we would not want circulated about ourselves. We give others the shadow of the doubt in questionable circumstances, as we would do for ourselves.

We discard all prejudices that we would resent as unfair if we were members of the race or group suffering discrimination. We respect, defend, and accept a person of any race, culture, or class as we wish to be regarded by them. We will love our neighbor as we love ourselves—and so fulfill Christ's second greatest commandment.

Christ rooted the commandment of reciprocity in what He called the first and greatest commandment. "Thou shalt love the Lord thy God with all thy heart, and with all thy soul, and with all thy mind" (Matthew 22:37, KJV). Then you will find in Him the strength to love your neighbor as yourself, taking even the second step—the mile-long step.

THE SECOND MILE

You just pulled your car to a stop at the train crossing, waiting for the 5:17 commuter to get stopped, unload, and quit blocking the street when you see, out of the corner of your eye, a kid coming down the hill on a bike. He's weaving and back-pedaling furiously, like his brakes just went out on him. Then you see that he can't help smashing into that train. You leap from your car as the bike hurtles by. It leaps the curbing and crumples against the slowly moving train, but the boy is thrown clear. He lands limply. It's obvious that he's hurt. Fortunate that there's a phone booth right there. With a few quick steps you're inside. You dial the emergency number. "Send the rescue squad," you order, and you snap out the address.

Back outside, you push through the gathering crowd. The boy's still unconscious. He's bleeding steadily from the leg. You look around desperately. "Is anybody here a doctor?" you demand. No answer. You listen for the ambulance. No sound. And the kid's bleeding to death, if he's still alive.

You know what to do. Get a compress on the leg, your medic training from service days tells you. Sure you know how. Just rip out your handkerchief, press it on the wound. You pull out the cloth and start toward the boy. Then someone in the crowd yells, "Don't you touch that kid. You move him and you may kill him. They'll sue you for everything you've got, mister." Well, you know all that, but you can see the blood running, and you can't just stand by and let his life drain away.

"Isn't there a doctor or a nurse here somewhere?" you shout again. No answer. How do you decide what to do?

The second mile is the most difficult journey we are ever asked to make. If you've ever played referee to a disagreement between equals of equal determination you've discovered its painfulness.

Once when negotiating a misunderstanding between two mature men—a disagreement that had begun in their profession but had seeped through into community, family, and church life—I first learned how long the second mile is.

First, I talked to one. "Look," he said, "I've bent over backward to settle this thing. I've gone the second and now the third mile, but he won't come an inch to meet me."

But the other man said, "I've already gone the second mile, and I'm not going an inch further."

One man had come two miles, the other three, and they were still miles apart. They were not even within shouting distance; at least, neither could hear the other.

But, actually, neither had begun even the first mile.

The first mile of duty. That mile marked "obligation."

Didn't each owe the other a listening ear to actually hear what the other was saying? An understanding mind to see why and what was in the other man's viewpoint? And a personal concern for the other's reputation?

Isn't the first mile the distance from blind self-defensiveness to sympathetic understanding of the other person? To come that first mile is nothing extra. It's only minimum humanity. No two persons are ever more than "two miles" apart. If they will each accept the obvious responsibility of one to another, they can and will meet.

"To walk the second mile" is a fascinating metaphor from Jesus Christ. The Roman government authorized its civil servants, postmen, and soldiers to commandeer free labor anywhere along the highway to help carry luggage and baggage, but only for one mile per person.

As a young man, Christ may have been impressed to carry a pack for the thousand paces specified as a Roman mile and, if no relief came in sight, may have been forced to carry it until another hapless citizen appeared. Obviously this law was less than popular.

But Jesus had the gall to say, "If anybody forces you to go a mile with him, do more—go two miles with him" (Matthew 5:41). What's worse, He also said, "If a man sues you in court and takes the shirt off your back, give him your coat too. If he slaps your face on one cheek, turn the other" (Matthew 5:39-40, paraphrase).

To sum up His teaching in simple words: Always live above the law. Do more than just "doing your duty." Aim higher than minimum living.

Live your forgiveness as a way of life—constantly and consistently.

To *live* forgiveness is to *give* wholehearted acceptance to others. There is no forgiveness without genuine acceptance of the other person as he or she is.

But it is more than a shallow acceptance that is nothing more than tolerance.

"Open your hearts to one another as Christ has opened his heart to you," Paul wrote to the Romans (Romans 15:7). To do this is to accept another in a way that takes real responsibility for the other. It is an accepting love that gets its sleeves rolled up and its hands dirty in helping, serving, lifting, and changing others' lives into the full freedom of forgiveness—God's forgiveness *and* ours.

Forgiveness is not leaving a person with the burden of "something to live down"—it is offering the other someone to live with! A friend like you.

But the greatest test of continual forgiveness is the daily kind of forgiving love that gives and takes, freely accepting the bruises and hurts of living—no matter how difficult the blows life deals us.

HOW DO YOU WANT TO BE TREATED?

Discover the joy of the second mile, the extra deed, the added service, the plus feature of love.

For the businessman facing a cutthroat competitor, he can refuse to respond with identical ruthlessness.

I once heard someone ask a Christian, "Why do you let that other businessman treat you so rudely?"

His answer? "I refuse to allow him and his attitudes to determine my behavior." That man knew the reward of plus-living.

Recently the head of a large corporation told me, "Yesterday, the president of one of the East's larger electric utility companies spent a whole morning negotiating a simple contract with me! 'We know your Christian principles,' he said to me, 'and we're worried that the contract might not be fair enough to you. Do you mind if we go over it once more to make sure your side is being upheld?' "

"Second-mile religion" is a matter of love. You've traveled the first mile when you've learned to love your friendly neighbor. You face the second mile when you decide to love your enemy, adversary, or competitor.

But second-mile love is not a matter of liking. It is a way of life. It is a new attitude toward others. It is a decision you make to desire the best for others—friend or enemy.

To love is to will and desire your neighbor's good whether you like him or not. The good Samaritan may not have liked the poor, beaten man in the ditch. But he acted in his behalf. He did something about the man's tragedy. "This," said Jesus, "is love."

Christian love is making the decision and taking the action that contributes to the welfare of others.

Such love is not dependent at all on the nature, the beauty, or the niceness of the one loved. It depends completely on the one doing the loving.

Love can be—and will be—emotional, because there are natural affections that rise in our hearts. But, far more, Christian love *(agape)* is volitional. It's a decision to seek the other's good.

Jesus does not command that we like our enemies with warm affection. We cannot always command our emotions. But we can command our actions. We can act lovingly toward others whether we like them or not.

This contradiction between feeling and choice, between emotion and volition, between liking and loving has been resolved in four different ways by Christians throughout the centuries.

The first is by defining Christian agape love as benevolence. It is shown in loving the unlovely and the unlovable in generous self-giving. This views love as a willing generosity and forgiveness as an undeserved gift. The second-mile behavior is based on the goodness of the lover. Yet this view belittles the beloved even in the act of loving. It is less than worthy of what Christ both taught and demonstrated.

The second solution is to define agape as willing obedience. It loves the other out of obedient altruism, out of duty and obligation to the commandment to love. This gives love a consistent vigor and stability, but it evokes resistance in the one loving and resentment in the one loved. No one feels affirmed by love given out of duty. Forgiveness, in this perspective, is an obligation owed if one is also to be forgiven.

The third solution is to love sacrificially. Agape is seen as willing self-sacrifice. In giving oneself, one expresses an unconditional love that accepts the other regardless of the cost. But self-sacrifice may be ultimately motivated by self-centeredness. "See how I ask nothing for myself; you always come first" is finally a statement of pride. Forgiveness, in this perspective, is substitutional, vicarious. The forgiver bears the pain of the other's act and his or her own anger and lets the other go free. This vertical forgiveness may be necessary in alienated acts of injury where no relationship has ever or will ever exist, but in ongoing relationships it is destructive.

The fourth solution is to love in equal regard. At this level of love, we prize others as having equal worth, as being loved by God to the extent that he or she was worth the cost of Calvary, as being made worthy by the presence of God within and among us. The teaching that we love our neighbor as ourself stretches from the Pentateuch to the Epistles. Equal regard values each person as an end in himself, as an irreducibly valuable being in herself. Forgiveness, seen in this light, is mutual, reciprocal, and two-way. It is reconciliation between persons who stand equally before God, whether they recognize it yet or not.

Agape, when seen as equal regard, can include all the previous definitions. It is benevolent—generous and inclusive—but it seeks to work itself out of this superior position as rapidly as possible. It is obedient, but not for the sake of obedience itself. It is self-sacrificial, but not out of righteous superiority. The motivation for self-sacrifice springs from a recognition of the worth of all persons. In taking this worth as ultimately important, it refuses to participate in violation of self or other. It sacrifices self in the interest of love emphasized by equal regard for all humankind.

How do you want to be treated? Do you want to be forgiven seventy times seven? Then, out of love, you will forgive and forgive and forgive again—seventy times seven.

Moody Press, a ministry of the Moody Bible Institute, is designed for education, evangelization, and edification. If we may assist you in knowing more about Christ and the Christian life, please write us without obligation: Moody Press, c/o MLM, Chicago, Illinois 60610.